Sun Tzu's Art of War

INTRODUCTION

In an era saturated with rapid technological advancements, the wisdom of an ancient Chinese military strategist might seem obsolete. But the principles outlined by Sun Tzu in «The Art of War» over two millennia ago remain relevant to this day. Beyond warfare, these teachings permeate disciplines like business, politics, sports, and personal development, underscoring their timeless value.

Sun Tzu, believed to have been a military general in the late Spring and Autumn Period of ancient China, crafted a work of literature and philosophy that transcends time and geography. «The Art of War,» composed of 13 chapters, each dedicated to a facet of warfare strategy, is not just a book—it's a roadmap to triumph in the face of conflict.

The purpose of this new edition of «The Art of War: Sun Tzu's Timeless Strategy» is to bring Sun Tzu's wisdom to a contemporary audience. In the spirit of making these teachings accessible, we have sought to present a clear and modern translation that stays true to the original text's intentions. Alongside this translation, we have included notes and commentary to illuminate Sun Tzu's cryptic axioms, giving readers a deeper understanding of the timeless wisdom contained within these pages.

This book is not just for the military enthusiast, the strategist, or the historian. It's for anyone who faces challenges and seeks to overcome them strategically, learning from one of the world's earliest and greatest strategists. As you explore the depths of this book, we hope that Sun Tzu's wisdom will provide you with new insights, challenge your perspectives, and inspire strategic thinking in all aspects of your life.

Whether you are navigating a battlefield, the corporate world, or the complex game of life itself, Sun Tzu's «The Art of War» offers guiding principles for your journey. Embark on this journey with an open mind and a receptive heart, for as Sun Tzu wrote, «In the midst of chaos, there is also opportunity.»

This is just the start of the book. Following the introduction, we would dive into the actual translated text of «The Art of War,» each chapter supplemented with notes and commentary, providing an enriched reading experience for the audience.

Chapter 1: Laying Plans/The Calculations

«The art of war is of vital importance to the State. It is a matter of life and death, a road either to safety or to ruin. Hence it is a subject of inquiry which can on no account be neglected.» - Sun Tzu

Sun Tzu begins his treatise by acknowledging the weighty significance of warfare for a state's survival and prosperity. It is not merely a series of armed conflicts but a matter of utmost national interest that can determine the life or death of a civilization. To neglect the art of war is to ignore a critical component of statecraft. In essence, this is not merely about warfare, but about strategic decision-making in the face of conflict and competition.

[Translator's Note]

Sun Tzu's opening sentence underlines the grave seriousness with which he approaches the subject. While the specific reference is to statecraft and warfare, these principles can be applied in various fields where strategic thinking and decision-making are required. Sun Tzu's wisdom has transcended time and geography, finding relevance in areas as diverse as business strategy, sports coaching, legal disputes, and political campaigns. The phrase «a road either to safety or to ruin» captures the high stakes inherent in strategic decision-making.

This is a beginning excerpt of Chapter 1, showcasing how the translated text of «The Art of War» will be accompanied by relevant commentary and translator's notes. The entire book would follow this format, bringing Sun Tzu's wisdom to a modern audience in a clear and understandable manner.

«The art of war, then, is governed by five constant factors, to be taken into account in one's deliberations, when seeking to determine the conditions obtaining in the field.» - Sun Tzu

Sun Tzu reveals that the complexity of warfare can be navigated through understanding and applying five key elements. These elements are not transient tactics but rather constant factors that hold true regardless of the specific circumstances. He implies that any military strategy must account for these factors in its planning and execution to secure victory.

[Translator's Note]

This reference to «five constant factors» sets the stage for Sun Tzu's detailed analysis of warfare. The «constant» nature of these factors emphasizes their fundamental role in strategic decision-making, asserting their relevance across different contexts and times. This principle is not limited to military operations alone. Whether we are considering business, sports, politics, or personal life decisions, these constant factors can help guide our strategy and actions.

«These are: (1) The Moral Law; (2) Heaven; (3) Earth; (4) The Commander; (5) Method and discipline.» - Sun Tzu

Sun Tzu lists the five constant factors that should govern the art of war. These factors represent various elements of warfare, from the moral authority that legitimizes a conflict, the physical environment within which it occurs, the leadership that directs it, to the methods and discipline that execute it.

[Translator's Note]

Sun Tzu's «five constant factors» are wide-ranging, reflecting the holistic view he takes of warfare. 'Moral Law' refers to the moral alignment and unity of the people. 'Heaven' and 'Earth' signify the natural conditions, including factors like weather, terrain, and timing. 'The Commander' embodies the leadership qualities required for successful command. Lastly, 'Method and discipline' refer to the organization, training, and control of military forces. When we transpose this concept to modern situations, these factors can be viewed as a comprehensive framework to analyze and resolve complex problems.

We would continue in this manner, going through each of Sun Tzu's teachings, translating them to modern language, and providing commentary to help readers apply these lessons in their lives. This first chapter sets the stage for understanding the deep strategic insights that will follow in the subsequent chapters.

«The Moral Law causes the people to be in complete accord with their ruler, so that they will follow him regardless of their lives, undismayed by any danger.» - Sun Tzu

Sun Tzu believes that the first constant factor, the Moral Law, is a crucial foundation for any successful military strategy. It denotes the importance of shared values and unity between a ruler and his people. This harmony ensures the people's willingness to follow their leader, even in the face of dire threats and danger.

[Translator's Note]

The 'Moral Law' as defined by Sun Tzu highlights the crucial role of leadership in creating a sense of shared purpose and moral alignment. In a modern context, this could be seen as the need for businesses, teams, or any group to have a clear and shared vision or mission. When individuals believe in the cause and trust their leader, they can collectively face challenges and strive towards their goals, even when the going gets tough.

«Heaven signifies night and day, cold and heat, times and seasons.» - Sun Tzu

Sun Tzu refers to 'Heaven' as the second constant factor, symbolizing natural elements and cycles like day and night, varying temperatures, and changing seasons. These are uncontrollable aspects that can significantly impact the outcomes of warfare and thus must be taken into account when strategizing.

[Translator's Note]

The 'Heaven' factor reflects Sun Tzu's recognition of the influence of natural forces and conditions on outcomes, despite human intentions and actions. In today's world, this could refer to understanding and adapting to external conditions and trends, such as market fluctuations, socio-political changes, or even literal weather conditions for certain industries. Effective strategy recognizes and incorporates these uncontrollable but predictable factors.

We would proceed along these lines, delving into each constant factor in detail, translating Sun Tzu's wisdom and providing commentary for modern understanding. The aim is to make this ancient strategy accessible and applicable to a variety of fields and challenges in today's world.

«Earth comprises distances, great and small; danger and security; open ground and narrow passes; the chances of life and death.» - Sun Tzu

Sun Tzu defines 'Earth' as the third constant factor, which stands for the physical and geographic conditions of the battlefield. These factors — such as terrain, distance, security, and possible paths — play a significant role in military strategy and can influence the likelihood of victory or defeat.

[Translator's Note]

'Earth' in modern contexts might refer to the physical, organizational, or market landscape in which we operate. This could include the logistical considerations of a supply chain, the competitive landscape in a business market, or the internal structure and communication channels within an organization. Understanding and navigating these physical and structural realities is a vital aspect of successful strategic planning.

«The Commander stands for the virtues of wisdom, sincerity, benevolence, courage, and strictness.» - Sun Tzu

Sun Tzu describes the 'Commander' as the fourth constant factor, emphasizing the qualities that an effective leader must embody. A leader's wisdom, sincerity, benevolence, courage, and strictness can profoundly impact the morale, discipline, and effectiveness of their forces.

[Translator's Note]

This principle remains relevant in today's leadership discourse, be it in a corporate, political, or social context. An effective leader needs wisdom to make sound decisions, sincerity to build trust, benevolence to inspire loyalty, courage to face challenges, and strictness to maintain discipline. Sun Tzu's list of virtues paints a picture of balanced leadership that fosters respect and allegiance, not through fear or coercion, but through character and conduct.

As the book progresses, each of these critical aspects will be expanded upon in detail, linking back to Sun Tzu's original insights and demonstrating how these ancient principles continue to inform successful strategy in our current times.

«Method and discipline are to be understood as the marshalling of the army in its proper subdivisions, the graduations of rank among the officers, the maintenance of roads by which supplies may reach the army, and the control of military expenditure.» - Sun Tzu

Finally, Sun Tzu presents 'Method and discipline' as the fifth constant factor. It encompasses the organization, logistics, and financial management of the military force. A successful military operation relies on well-structured ranks, maintained supply lines, and controlled expenses.

[Translator's Note]

In today's terms, 'Method and discipline' could be seen as the operational efficiency and financial prudence in an organization. A successful entity must maintain clear lines of communication, effective logistical systems, and efficient use of resources. Sun Tzu's focus on this aspect reaffirms that strategy isn't just about high-level decision-making; it's also about the tactical execution and disciplined operations that bring the strategy to life.

«These five heads should be familiar to every general: he who knows them will be victorious; he who knows them not will fail.» - Sun Tzu

Sun Tzu ends this section by reinforcing the importance of these five constant factors in determining the outcome of any military endeavor. Knowledge of these factors is not just advantageous, but critical to achieving victory.

[Translator's Note]

This concluding sentence underscores the universal applicability and critical importance of these five factors. Whether you're a business leader, a sports coach, a political strategist, or simply someone trying to navigate personal challenges, understanding these factors can equip you with the insights necessary to strategize effectively and triumph over your difficulties.

This completion of the first chapter sets the foundation for the exploration of Sun Tzu's strategic wisdom in the following chapters. The consistent format of translation and commentary ensures that readers grasp the essence of these timeless teachings and can relate them to their own experiences and challenges.

Chapter 2: Waging War/The Challenge

«When you engage in actual fighting, if victory is long in coming, then men's weapons will grow dull and their ardor will be dampened. If you lay siege to a city, you will exhaust your strength.»
- Sun Tzu

Sun Tzu highlights the dangers of protracted conflict in this opening statement of the chapter. Long-drawn battles not only drain physical resources like weapons but also diminish the morale and enthusiasm of the warriors. Even the most fortified city will sap your strength if besieged for too long.

[Translator's Note]

This ancient wisdom is highly relevant today in any competitive environment, whether it be business, politics, or even personal matters. The cost of extended conflict is high, often resulting in diminished morale, loss of momentum, and wasted resources. Strategists are hence advised to seek swift and decisive victories, efficiently solving disputes or achieving objectives.

«Again, if the campaign is protracted, the resources of the State will not be equal to the strain.» - Sun Tzu

Sun Tzu further asserts that long-lasting conflicts can be unsustainable for a state's resources. The prolonged deployment of manpower, weapons, and other assets can stress the state's capacity and ultimately weaken its position.

[Translator's Note]

Sun Tzu here points to the fact that resources are always finite, and their judicious use is crucial to any strategy. A modern equivalent would be the drain on financial, human, or even time resources during a long-lasting project or business competition. This emphasizes the importance of efficiency and time management in strategic planning.

Chapter 2 continues to explore the intricacies of waging war, emphasizing the importance of managing resources, understanding the cost of conflict, and the strategy of efficient victories. We continue to elucidate Sun Tzu's principles and explain their application in a modern context.

«Now, when your weapons are dulled, your ardor dampened, your strength exhausted and your treasure spent, other chieftains will spring up to take advantage of your extremity. Then no man, however wise, will be able to avert the consequences that must ensue.» - Sun Tzu

Sun Tzu warns of the consequences of prolonged warfare. He paints a picture of weakened forces, diminished morale, exhausted resources, and a vulnerable state ripe for exploitation by opportunistic foes. In such a scenario, even the wisest leader would be hard-pressed to prevent disaster.

[Translator's Note]

This stark warning is a timeless reminder of the vulnerabilities that can arise from over-extension, whether in warfare, business, or personal endeavors. An organization stretched thin may become a target for competition, a leader may lose credibility, or an individual may burn out. It emphasizes the importance of strategic resource management and the dangers of overreaching without adequate preparation or sustainability.

«Thus, though we have heard of stupid haste in war, cleverness has never been seen associated with long delays.» - Sun Tzu

Sun Tzu contrasts the folly of rushed action with the misconception that prolonged delays equate to strategic wisdom. While reckless speed can lead to mistakes, a protracted process doesn't necessarily reflect intelligent planning.

[Translator's Note]

Sun Tzu's wisdom dispels the notion that longer means better when it comes to strategy. The key lies in effective and timely decision-making, avoiding both hasty blunders and wasted opportunities due to excessive delay. This principle can apply to decision-making in any field, underlining the importance of balance between speed and caution.

As we proceed with Chapter 2, Sun Tzu's timeless strategies continue to unfold, providing insights into effective resource management, strategic timing, and the judicious balance between haste and delay. Our commentary aims to make these principles accessible and applicable to various modern contexts.

«There is no instance of a country having benefited from prolonged warfare.» - Sun Tzu

Sun Tzu declares unequivocally that no state has ever benefited from drawn-out conflict. This reinforces his stance on the cost of war and the necessity of strategizing for swift and decisive victories.

[Translator's Note]

This principle underlines the overarching theme that avoiding unnecessary expenditure of resources is central to effective strategy. In a modern context, this could be seen as a reminder to businesses to avoid drawn-out competitive battles, to policy-makers to resolve disputes efficiently, or to individuals to not let personal conflicts fester.

«It is only one who is thoroughly acquainted with the evils of war that can thoroughly understand the profitable way of carrying it on.» - Sun Tzu

Sun Tzu believes that a deep understanding of the consequences and costs of warfare is essential to lead a profitable campaign. Those who truly comprehend the toll it takes can strategize the most effective and least damaging way to wage war.

[Translator's Note]

This statement highlights the importance of fully understanding the potential negative impacts before embarking on any strategic action. This not only includes wars but also any decision that may have significant repercussions, such as business investments, policy decisions, or personal life choices. It serves as a reminder to always weigh the pros and cons carefully, understanding the possible 'evils' before committing to action.

As we move deeper into Chapter 2, the complexities and nuances of strategic planning according to Sun Tzu are further explored. We continue to relate these age-old principles to contemporary scenarios, making them relevant and practical for today's reader.

«The skillful soldier does not raise a second levy, neither are his supply wagons loaded more than twice.» - Sun Tzu

Sun Tzu emphasizes the competence of a skillful soldier by highlighting their efficiency in resource management. He suggests that they do not require multiple levies of troops nor more than two rounds of supply collection, underlining the importance of planning and preparation.

[Translator's Note]

Sun Tzu's wisdom here points to the concept of doing things right the first time. In a modern context, this could apply to business planning, where efficient operations aim to minimize redundancy and waste. It suggests that competent planning can save resources, time, and effort, and is a key aspect of any successful strategy.

«Bring war material with you from home, but forage on the enemy. Thus the army will have food enough for its needs.» - Sun Tzu

Sun Tzu advises bringing necessary war material from home but using the enemy's resources for sustenance wherever possible. This not only conserves your own resources but also can demoralize and weaken the enemy.

[Translator's Note]

In today's terms, this principle might translate to utilizing existing resources while strategically tapping into external opportunities to preserve your own assets. In a business context, this could mean exploring partnerships, collaborations, or mergers to gain resources and advantages, all while conserving internal assets.

Chapter 2 continues to unpack the complexities of waging war, illustrating the importance of efficient resource management and strategic planning. Our translations and commentaries aim to make these ancient strategies relatable and applicable to a wide array of modern challenges.

«Poverty of the State exchequer causes an army to be maintained by contributions from a distance. Contributing to maintain an army at a distance causes the people to be impoverished.» - Sun Tzu

Sun Tzu warns against the negative cycle of maintaining an army through contributions from afar. He notes that when a state's coffers are low, it often results in the people being burdened with sustaining the army, leading to widespread impoverishment.

[Translator's Note]

This is an age-old caution against the dangers of overextending resources and the ripple effects it can have on a community or organization. In the modern context, overextension might refer to spending beyond one's means, whether in business expansion, government expenditure, or personal finances. Sun Tzu reminds us of the need for financial prudence and sustainability in all strategic considerations.

«On the other hand, the proximity of an army causes prices to go up; and high prices cause the people's substance to be drained away.» - Sun Tzu

Sun Tzu observes that having an army nearby also has negative consequences. It can lead to inflation, and this, in turn, diminishes people's wealth.

[Translator's Note]

Here, Sun Tzu touches upon the economic implications of military action, a lesson that could apply to any situation causing disruption to the local economy. It's a reminder that large-scale actions often have wider, indirect impacts that need to be considered in strategic planning.

As we continue our journey through Sun Tzu's Art of War, Chapter 2 provides valuable lessons on the economic and societal implications of warfare, and by extension, any significant strategic action. The translations and commentaries aim to extract relevant insights for application in various modern scenarios.

«When their substance is drained away, the peasantry will be afflicted by heavy exactions. With this loss of substance and exhaustion of strength, the homes of the people will be stripped bare, and three-tenths of their income will be dissipated.» - Sun Tzu

Sun Tzu goes on to describe the adverse effects of military campaigns on the general populace. The depletion of resources and strength, heavy taxes, and the reduction of income lead to significant hardships for the people.

[Translator's Note]

Sun Tzu's words serve as a stark reminder of the real-world consequences of large-scale strategic decisions. In a modern context, this can be a caution against the fallout from major policy decisions, business strategies, or economic measures that might negatively impact communities or society at large. The importance of holistic, considerate planning is underlined here.

«While government expenses for broken chariots, worn-out horses, breast-plates and helmets, bows and arrows, spears and shields, protective mantles, draught-oxen and heavy wagons, will amount to four-tenths of its total revenue.» - Sun Tzu

Sun Tzu concludes this section with an examination of the government's expenditure during war times. He estimates that nearly 40% of the total revenue is spent on repairing and replacing war equipment, illustrating the heavy financial burden of war.

[Translator's Note]

Sun Tzu provides a concrete sense of the economic cost of warfare or, in a broader sense, any major undertaking. In modern terms, these costs might be analogous to the capital expenditures or operating costs incurred by organizations. It's a stark reminder to always consider the full financial implications and potential unexpected costs associated with any significant decision or project.

Through Sun Tzu's Art of War, readers are encouraged to view strategic decision-making with a wide lens, considering not just the immediate gains but also the potential long-term costs and impacts.

«Hence a wise general makes a point of foraging on the enemy. One cartload of the enemy's provisions is equivalent to twenty of one's own, and likewise a single picul of his provender is equivalent to twenty from one's own store.» - Sun Tzu

Sun Tzu introduces the concept of utilizing enemy resources to lighten the burden on one's own provisions. He argues that one unit of the enemy's provisions is worth twenty of one's own, underscoring the dual advantage of conserving your resources while depleting the enemy's.

[Translator's Note]

This strategy speaks to the idea of leveraging opportunities in your external environment to minimize costs and maximize gains. In modern business terms, this could apply to scenarios like making use of a competitor's weak point, capitalizing on market trends, or leveraging partnerships to boost your own resources.

«In order to kill the enemy, our men must be roused to anger; that there may be advantage from defeating the enemy, they must have their rewards.» - Sun Tzu

Sun Tzu highlights the importance of motivation in achieving victory. He argues that to effectively face the enemy, soldiers must be driven by anger, and to see benefits from defeating the enemy, they must be incentivized with rewards.

[Translator's Note]

Sun Tzu's insight can be generalized to understand the motivational factors in any team setting. In business, sports, or any group effort, the team must be emotionally invested (roused to anger) and see clear benefits (have their rewards) to give their best performance.

Chapter 2's exploration of warfare strategy continues, providing valuable insights into resource management and team motivation. Through translation and commentary, we strive to make these ancient principles relevant and actionable in today's world.

«Therefore in chariot fighting, when ten or more chariots have been taken, those should be rewarded who took the first. Our own flags should be substituted for those of the enemy, and the chariots mingled and used in conjunction with ours. The captured soldiers should be kindly treated and kept.» - Sun Tzu

Sun Tzu advises rewarding those who are the first to seize enemy chariots, suggesting the replacement of enemy flags with our own, and integrating captured equipment into our forces. He also emphasizes humane treatment of captured soldiers.

[Translator's Note]

These principles highlight the importance of reward systems in recognizing first movers or high performers, and the strategic value of reutilizing captured resources. Additionally, Sun Tzu's advice to treat captured soldiers kindly may be interpreted today as the importance of empathy and respect even in competitive situations.

«This is called, using the conquered foe to augment one's own strength.» - Sun Tzu

Sun Tzu encapsulates these strategies under the concept of using the conquered foe to increase one's strength. This includes both tangible resources and the potential loyalty of the captured soldiers.

[Translator's Note]

Sun Tzu's wisdom here emphasizes leveraging all available resources, even those gained from competitors, to strengthen your own position. In a modern context, it could relate to acquiring assets from competitors, absorbing another company's client base after a merger, or even learning from the mistakes of rivals to avoid similar pitfalls.

As we conclude Chapter 2, Sun Tzu's strategies continue to offer relevant lessons on resource management, humaneness in conflict, and strategic use of advantages. These timeless principles find applications in various aspects of modern life, from business and politics to personal development.

Chapter 3: Planning Offensives

«In the practical art of war, the best thing of all is to take the enemy's country whole and intact; to shatter and destroy it is not so good.» - Sun Tzu

Sun Tzu opens this chapter by stating that the ultimate victory in warfare is to conquer the enemy's country whole and intact. He argues against wanton destruction, suggesting that preserving the enemy's resources offers greater strategic value.

[Translator's Note]

This perspective emphasizes the importance of strategic foresight over short-term triumph. In a modern context, it reminds us to consider the long-term value of our actions, whether in business mergers, political negotiations, or personal decisions.

«So, too, it is better to recapture an army entire than to destroy it, to capture a regiment, a detachment or a company entire than to destroy them.» - Sun Tzu

Sun Tzu extends this principle to the capture of enemy forces. He suggests that it is more advantageous to capture an enemy unit intact rather than destroying it, once again underscoring the value of preservation over destruction.

[Translator's Note]

This ancient wisdom applies in situations where the goal is to not only win but also gain something from the victory. This could be seen in today's corporate world where, for instance, acquiring a competitor may be more advantageous than driving them out of business entirely.

Chapter 3, «Planning Offensives», starts with Sun Tzu's emphasis on the strategic advantage of preservation over destruction. Through our translations and commentaries, we aim to illustrate the applicability of these principles in various contexts today.

«Hence to fight and conquer in all your battles is not supreme excellence; supreme excellence consists in breaking the enemy's resistance without fighting.» - Sun Tzu

Sun Tzu states that the highest form of warfare is not to win every battle through combat but to break the enemy's resistance without even having to fight.

[Translator's Note]

This thought-provoking statement reflects the idea that the most effective strategies are those that achieve desired outcomes with minimal conflict or resource expenditure. In a modern context, this might refer to diplomatic resolutions, effective negotiations, or innovative business strategies that outmaneuver competition without direct confrontation.

«Thus the highest form of generalship is to balk the enemy's plans; the next best is to prevent the junction of the enemy's forces; the next in order is to attack the enemy's army in the field; and the worst policy of all is to besiege walled cities.» - Sun Tzu

Sun Tzu categorizes various forms of generalship, ranking them from the most desirable (thwarting the enemy's plans) to the least desirable (laying siege to walled cities). Each strategy requires varying levels of resources and poses different risks.

[Translator's Note]

Sun Tzu's wisdom could be applied to any situation where there are different potential strategies, each with varying levels of risk and resource investment. For example, in business, the highest form of strategy might be to innovate and create a market where none existed, thereby «balking» the plans of potential competitors. On the other end, the least desirable strategy might involve direct competition in a highly saturated market.

Chapter 3 continues to explore the art of strategic planning and decision-making. By interpreting Sun Tzu's lessons, we aim to offer valuable insights applicable to a variety of contemporary scenarios.

«The rule is, not to besiege walled cities if it can possibly be avoided. The preparation of mantlets, movable shelters, and various implements of war, will take up three whole months; and the piling up of mounds over against the walls will take three months more.» - Sun Tzu

Sun Tzu advises against laying siege to walled cities, as it involves a significant investment of time and resources. He estimates that the preparations alone could take up to half a year, underscoring the inefficiency of this approach.

[Translator's Note]

In a contemporary context, this advice can be seen as a warning against tackling challenges head-on when they are heavily fortified or resistant to change. Whether in business, diplomacy, or personal life, sometimes it may be wiser to search for less direct, more creative solutions.

«The general, unable to control his irritation, will launch his men to the assault like swarming ants, with the result that one-third of his men are slain, while the town still remains untaken. Such are the disastrous effects of a siege.» - Sun Tzu

Sun Tzu describes the potential consequences of a siege, including heavy losses and the potential failure to capture the city. He warns against letting frustration dictate strategy, resulting in disastrous outcomes.

[Translator's Note]

This insight warns against the pitfalls of impatience and frustration, reminding us that decisions driven by negative emotions often lead to poor outcomes. In a modern context, this can be a crucial lesson for any leader or decision-maker.

Sun Tzu's wisdom in Chapter 3 provides guidance on strategic decision-making, emphasizing patience, planning, and control over impulsive actions. As we translate and interpret these teachings, we aim to extract lessons applicable to our lives today.

«Therefore the skillful leader subdues the enemy's troops without any fighting; he captures their cities without laying siege to them; he overthrows their kingdom without lengthy operations in the field.» - Sun Tzu

Sun Tzu asserts that the most adept leaders can achieve their objectives without resorting to violent conflict, exhausting sieges, or long-term military operations. They manage to subdue the enemy, capture cities, and overthrow kingdoms with strategies that avoid direct confrontation and protracted warfare.

[Translator's Note]

This passage underscores the value of strategic ingenuity, diplomacy, and non-violent means of conflict resolution. Whether in international relations, business competition, or interpersonal disputes, the goal is often best achieved not through direct confrontation but through clever strategy, negotiation, and persuasion.

«With his forces intact he will dispute the mastery of the Empire, and thus, without losing a man, his triumph will be complete. This is the method of attacking by stratagem.» - Sun Tzu

Sun Tzu concludes that with his forces preserved and morale high, a clever leader can compete for supremacy. Without sacrificing a single life, his victory is complete through the use of strategic cunning rather than brute force.

[Translator's Note]

Sun Tzu's wisdom resonates in various aspects of modern life. It highlights the importance of careful planning, the preservation of resources, and the value of achieving objectives through intelligent strategy over brute force. In today's world, these lessons can be applied in everything from business negotiations to environmental conservation.

Chapter 3 of Sun Tzu's Art of War continues to provide timeless insights into effective strategy and leadership. As we extract and interpret these teachings, we aim to offer modern readers relevant applications for these ancient principles.

Chapter 4: Tactical Dispositions

«The good fighters of old first put themselves beyond the possibility of defeat, and then waited for an opportunity of defeating the enemy.» - Sun Tzu

Sun Tzu begins this chapter by describing the methods of successful warriors of the past. They ensured their own security before seeking opportunities to defeat the enemy.

[Translator's Note]

This principle encourages us to secure our own position before engaging in offensive actions. In a modern context, this could mean ensuring a solid financial foundation before investing in risky ventures, or building a strong product and reputation before branching out into new markets.

«To secure ourselves against defeat lies in our own hands, but the opportunity of defeating the enemy is provided by the enemy himself.» - Sun Tzu

Sun Tzu argues that while we control our own defense, the ability to defeat the enemy depends largely on the enemy's actions. Essentially, our protection is in our control, but exploiting an enemy's weaknesses relies on their mistakes.

[Translator's Note]

This statement stresses the importance of focusing on factors within our control while staying alert to opportunities that may arise from external circumstances. For instance, in business, a company should focus on improving its product, services, and operational efficiency, while keeping an eye on market trends and competitors' weaknesses.

The fourth chapter, «Tactical Dispositions», begins by exploring the importance of self-preservation and the exploitation of enemy weaknesses in warfare. Through our translations and commentaries, we aim to bring these ancient lessons to life in contemporary scenarios.

«Thus the good fighter is able to secure himself against defeat, but cannot make certain of defeating the enemy.» - Sun Tzu

Sun Tzu notes that a good fighter can secure himself against defeat, but victory over the enemy isn't guaranteed. This distinction underscores the importance of defense and the uncertain nature of offense.

[Translator's Note]

This observation holds true for various situations today, where a solid defense (in business, this might be a strong brand, unique products, or excellent customer service) is often easier to control than the offense (new market penetration, for instance, which depends on numerous external factors).

«Hence the saying: One may know how to conquer without being able to do it.» - Sun Tzu

Sun Tzu emphasizes the difference between knowing how to win and being able to achieve it. This highlights the gap between knowledge and application, a common challenge in all domains of life.

[Translator's Note]

This wisdom can apply to many modern situations. For instance, a team might understand the strategy to win a game, a business might know the market dynamics to capture a new segment, or an individual might know the path to personal improvement. However, knowing does not guarantee successful execution, which requires planning, preparation, skill, and sometimes a bit of luck.

Chapter 4 continues to offer invaluable insights into the nature of defense and offense, the gap between knowledge and action, and the importance of execution. Through translation and commentary, these ancient strategies are brought into a modern context.

«Security against defeat implies defensive tactics; ability to defeat the enemy means taking the offensive.» - Sun Tzu

Sun Tzu explains that protection against defeat involves defensive strategies, whereas the ability to defeat the enemy necessitates offensive action. This delineates the roles of defense and offense in warfare.

[Translator's Note]

The balance between defense and offense is relevant in many aspects of modern life, from sports to business to personal development. For instance, a company must balance defensive strategies (such as protecting intellectual property and maintaining market share) with offensive strategies (like innovation and expansion).

«Standing on the defensive indicates insufficient strength; attacking, a superabundance of strength.» - Sun Tzu

Sun Tzu suggests that defensive posture indicates a lack of strength, while an offensive approach signals an abundance of strength. This view associates the defensive stance with weakness and the offensive stance with power.

[Translator's Note]

This statement, while potentially controversial, speaks to the perception of power in competitive situations. In business, for example, a company that is always in defensive mode might be perceived as weak or struggling, while one that continually innovates and pushes new initiatives may be seen as strong and thriving.

Through the lens of Chapter 4, Sun Tzu provides strategic insights into the balance of defense and offense, and the perceptions of power in competition. These timeless principles continue to resonate in a variety of modern scenarios.

«The general who is skilled in defense hides in the most secret recesses of the earth; he who is skilled in attack flashes forth from the topmost heights of heaven. Thus on the one hand we have ability to protect ourselves; on the other, a victory that is complete.» - Sun Tzu

Sun Tzu emphasizes the strategic locations from which a skilled general operates when on defense or offense. He correlates the art of defense with secrecy and the art of attack with unexpected, swift action.

[Translator's Note]

The metaphorical use of «recesses of the earth» and «heights of heaven» can be interpreted in modern contexts as well. It speaks to the notion of choosing the right positioning depending on whether you are on the defensive or offensive side. For instance, in business, a defensive strategy might involve careful resource allocation and risk mitigation, whereas an offensive strategy might involve aggressive marketing and innovation.

«To see victory only when it is within the ken of the common herd is not the acme of excellence.» - Sun Tzu

Sun Tzu suggests that seeing victory only when it is obvious to all is not the hallmark of exceptional leadership. A truly great leader is able to perceive victory in its nascent stages, well before it becomes apparent to others.

[Translator's Note]

This wisdom is as true today as it was during Sun Tzu's time. In business, it might refer to the ability of visionary leaders to foresee the potential success of a product, service, or market trend long before others can. This foresight is what sets apart the great innovators and entrepreneurs of our time.

Chapter 4 of Sun Tzu's Art of War, titled «Tactical Dispositions», continues to shed light on the intricate dance between defense and offense, the importance of perception, and the value of foresight. Through our translations and commentaries, we aim to provide valuable, applicable lessons for modern readers.

«Neither is it the acme of excellence if you fight and conquer and the whole Empire says, 'Well done!'» - Sun Tzu

Sun Tzu further argues that achieving victory in a way that everybody expects is not the pinnacle of excellence. The true excellence, he implies, lies in outthinking the enemy, achieving objectives without unnecessary conflict.

[Translator's Note]

This perspective promotes the value of unconventional thinking and strategy. It's not about winning the way everyone expects, but about finding new, innovative paths to victory. For instance, in the business world, the most admired victories often come from disruptive companies that change the status quo, not from those who merely do what is expected.

«To lift an autumn hair is no sign of great strength; to see the sun and moon is no sign of sharp sight; to hear the noise of thunder is no sign of a quick ear.» - Sun Tzu

Sun Tzu draws upon simple metaphors to convey that performing easy tasks or recognizing obvious things is not a sign of strength, sharp sight, or quick hearing. True ability lies in performing challenging tasks and recognizing subtleties that others miss.

[Translator's Note]

This wisdom speaks to the value of subtlety, discernment, and the ability to do what others find difficult. Today, it's not the easy victories that determine true success in any field, but rather the ability to tackle complex challenges and uncover hidden opportunities.

Through Chapter 4, Sun Tzu guides us on the importance of innovative strategies, discernment, and the ability to perform difficult tasks. These lessons remain remarkably relevant, providing insights applicable to various modern contexts.

«What the ancients called a clever fighter is one who not only wins, but excels in winning with ease.» - Sun Tzu

Sun Tzu outlines what constitutes a 'clever fighter' in the eyes of the ancients: not just someone who secures victory, but who does so effortlessly. This emphasizes the value of strategic brilliance over brute force.

[Translator's Note]

In our contemporary world, the 'clever fighters' are often those who find smarter, more efficient ways to succeed. In the business context, this could be seen in companies who disrupt industries with innovative technologies or business models, winning market share with seeming ease.

«Hence his victories bring him neither reputation for wisdom nor credit for courage.» - Sun Tzu

Sun Tzu suggests that the clever fighter's victories do not earn him a reputation for wisdom or courage because his victories seem effortless and not born out of traditional brute force or bravery.

[Translator's Note]

This paradoxical statement underscores that true mastery can often go unrecognized because it makes the difficult seem easy. In modern terms, think of technology innovators who drastically simplify user experience. Their work is often not appreciated for the complex processes that run behind the scenes, because they make it seem so effortless to the end-user.

Chapter 4, «Tactical Dispositions», continues to delve into the concept of strategic brilliance and the value of making victory seem effortless. These timeless principles find their applications in various facets of our modern lives.

«He wins his battles by making no mistakes. Making no mistakes is what establishes the certainty of victory, for it means conquering an enemy that is already defeated.» - Sun Tzu

Sun Tzu posits that the key to victory lies in making no mistakes, essentially fighting an enemy who is already defeated. This strategy highlights the importance of flawless execution and proactive measures that put the enemy at a disadvantage before the battle even begins.

[Translator's Note]

In modern times, this could translate to a company strategically positioning itself in such a way that it has the upper hand against its competitors even before the competition begins. This might involve preemptive measures such as securing key partnerships, patents, or technologies that would give the company a significant advantage.

«Hence the skillful fighter puts himself into a position which makes defeat impossible, and does not miss the moment for defeating the enemy.» - Sun Tzu

Sun Tzu advises that a skillful fighter positions himself in a way that makes defeat impossible while also seizing the right moment to defeat the enemy. This illustrates the dual importance of both defensive and offensive strategies in warfare.

Applied today, this could refer to the balance between building a strong defense (e.g., a robust business model, a dedicated customer base) and identifying the right moment to go on the offensive (e.g., entering new markets, launching new products).

In this part of Chapter 4, Sun Tzu discusses the importance of strategic positioning and seizing opportunities, offering timeless wisdom that continues to find resonance in various fields of modern life.

«Thus it is that in war the victorious strategist only seeks battle after the victory has been won, whereas he who is destined to defeat first fights and afterwards looks for victory.» - Sun Tzu

Sun Tzu conveys that the victorious strategist only engages in battle after securing the conditions for victory. In contrast, those destined for defeat rush into battle and then seek victory. This emphasizes the importance of strategic preparation and foresight in winning battles.

[Translator's Note]

This strategic wisdom can be applied to many situations in the modern world. For instance, a successful business might only enter a new market after thorough research and groundwork have established a strong likelihood of success. In contrast, a less successful business might rush into a new market without sufficient preparation, hoping to figure things out along the way.

«The consummate leader cultivates the moral law, and strictly adheres to method and discipline; thus it is in his power to control success.» - Sun Tzu

Sun Tzu closes the chapter with an emphasis on the moral law, method, and discipline. A great leader has the power to control success by adhering to these principles.

[Translator's Note]

The «moral law» mentioned by Sun Tzu may translate into modern contexts as ethical conduct or corporate responsibility. The reference to method and discipline speaks to the importance of consistent processes and strict adherence to established guidelines. These principles remain crucial in successful leadership today.

With this, we conclude Chapter 4, «Tactical Dispositions», of Sun Tzu's Art of War. This chapter offers numerous lessons on strategy, preparation, and leadership that remain relevant in various facets of contemporary life.

Chapter 5: «Energy»

This chapter will explore the concept of «energy» in a military context, which essentially refers to the way in which a military force is deployed and managed. It discusses various strategies and tactics for harnessing and directing energy effectively to ensure victory.

Content Breakdown:
1. The Dual Nature of Energy: Direct and Indirect Methods.
2. The Interplay of Direct and Indirect Energy: The 'Infinite Repercussions' of Military Actions.
3. Deception and Energy: The Role of Deception in Military Strategy.
4. The Flexible and Ever-Changing Nature of Energy.
5. Strategic Application of Energy: Choosing When to Fight.
6. Energy and Timing: The Importance of Timing in Military Engagements.
7. Harnessing the Enemy's Energy: Turning the Enemy's Strengths into Weaknesses.
8. Conservation of Energy: The Importance of Preserving One's Strength in War.
9. Utilization of Energy in Different Situations: Deploying Energy to Deal with Different Terrain and Situations.
10. The Role of the Leader in Directing Energy.

«Sun Tzu said: The control of a large force is the same principle as the control of a few men: it is merely a question of dividing up their numbers.» - Sun Tzu

Sun Tzu starts the chapter by stating that controlling a large force operates on the same principle as controlling a small group. The key lies in effective division and management of numbers.

[Translator's Note]

This is an enduring principle that translates well into modern contexts. It can be seen in how large corporations manage thousands of employees by breaking them down into manageable teams or departments. Similarly, in project management, large tasks are often divided into smaller, manageable parts to ensure effective execution.

«Fighting with a large army under your command is nowise different from fighting with a small one: it is merely a question of instituting signs and signals.» - Sun Tzu

Sun Tzu continues by suggesting that the challenge of leading a large army is the same as leading a small one. The solution lies in establishing effective communication systems, such as signs and signals.

[Translator's Note]

Communication is key in any organization, large or small. In today's businesses, effective communication strategies and technologies are crucial to coordinate teams, especially in the era of remote and distributed workforces.

Sun Tzu's opening statements in Chapter 5 «Energy», emphasize the importance of organization, management, and communication in commanding forces, principles that remain relevant and applicable in the modern world.

«To ensure that your whole host may withstand the brunt of the enemy's attack and remain unshaken - this is effected by maneuvers direct and indirect.» - Sun Tzu

Sun Tzu notes that to ensure the entire army can withstand enemy attacks and remain firm, one must employ both direct and indirect maneuvers.

[Translator's Note]

In a modern context, this could be interpreted as the need for a combination of direct and indirect strategies to achieve objectives. For instance, a business might employ direct strategies like competitive pricing and indirect strategies like brand building to capture and maintain market share.

«That the impact of your army may be like a grindstone dashed against an egg - this is effected by the science of weak points and strong.» - Sun Tzu

Sun Tzu compares the ideal impact of an army to a grindstone dashed against an egg, highlighting the need to understand the science of weak points and strong.

[Translator's Note]

This speaks to the necessity of understanding and exploiting vulnerabilities while reinforcing strengths in any competitive scenario. For example, in business, this might involve identifying a competitor's weaknesses and designing strategies to exploit them while simultaneously reinforcing one's own unique strengths.

Through the opening verses of Chapter 5 «Energy», Sun Tzu draws attention to the importance of direct and indirect maneuvers and understanding strengths and weaknesses, offering timeless lessons for contemporary readers.

«In all fighting, the direct method may be used for joining battle, but indirect methods will be needed in order to secure victory.» - Sun Tzu

Sun Tzu notes that while direct methods may be used to engage in battle, indirect methods are often required to secure victory. This emphasizes the need for subtlety and strategy in achieving success.

[Translator's Note]

This principle applies in many contemporary situations. For instance, a company might use direct methods to compete (like matching a competitor's pricing), but indirect methods (like building customer loyalty through superior service) may ultimately determine who wins in the market.

«Indirect tactics, efficiently applied, are inexhaustible as Heaven and Earth, unending as the flow of rivers and streams; like the sun and moon, they end but to begin anew; like the four seasons, they pass away to return once more.» - Sun Tzu

Sun Tzu likens the power of indirect tactics to the inexhaustible and cyclical nature of heaven and earth, rivers and streams, and the sun and moon. This underscores the enduring value of smart, strategic action.

[Translator's Note]

This timeless wisdom emphasizes the enduring power of strategic, indirect action - a principle that remains relevant in many fields today, from business to politics to social change. For example, a social media campaign (an indirect tactic) can have a powerful, long-lasting impact on public opinion and behavior.

In these portions of Chapter 5, «Energy,» Sun Tzu highlights the enduring value of indirect tactics and strategic subtlety, offering valuable lessons that resonate with modern readers.

«There are not more than five musical notes, yet the combinations of these five give rise to more melodies than can ever be heard.» - Sun Tzu

Sun Tzu uses the metaphor of musical notes to illustrate that there are endless possibilities even with a limited number of elements. This underscores the importance of creativity and adaptability in strategy.

[Translator's Note]

This metaphor holds true in numerous contemporary situations. In business, for instance, there may be a limited number of marketing techniques or technologies, but the ways in which these can be combined and adapted are virtually limitless, leading to an infinite array of potential strategies.

«There are not more than five primary colors, yet in combination they produce more hues than can ever be seen.» - Sun Tzu

Again, Sun Tzu uses the metaphor of primary colors to stress the infinite possibilities that arise from a limited number of elements when they are creatively combined.

[Translator's Note]

This principle is evident in areas like product development where a limited set of components or features can be combined in numerous ways to create a wide variety of unique and innovative products.

In these passages from Chapter 5, «Energy,» Sun Tzu emphasizes the power of creativity and combination in strategy, using metaphors that remain profoundly relevant for modern readers in diverse fields.

«There are not more than five cardinal tastes; yet combinations of them yield more flavors than can ever be tasted.» - Sun Tzu

Sun Tzu completes his metaphor trilogy - music, colors, and now tastes - to further stress the endless possibilities that arise from creatively combining a limited number of elements.

[Translator's Note]

This example can be applied to any situation where a limited set of resources can be combined to create endless possibilities. For instance, a chef might use only a few basic ingredients but can create an astonishing variety of dishes by combining them in different ways.

«In battle, there are not more than two methods of attack: the direct and the indirect; yet these two in combination give rise to an endless series of maneuvers.» - Sun Tzu

Sun Tzu circles back to warfare, pointing out that although there are only two methods of attack (direct and indirect), these can be combined to create a virtually endless array of maneuvers.

[Translator's Note]

In the business world, this principle holds true as well. Direct methods (such as overt competition) and indirect methods (like strategic alliances or mergers) can be combined in countless ways to adapt to various market conditions and achieve business objectives.

In this part of Chapter 5, «Energy», Sun Tzu stresses the concept of combining elements in strategy, offering profound insights for contemporary readers in various fields.

«The quality of decision is like the well-timed swoop of a falcon which enables it to strike and destroy its victim.» - Sun Tzu

Sun Tzu compares a well-made decision to a well-timed falcon swoop, emphasizing the significance of timing in decision-making and its potential to ensure victory.

[Translator's Note]

Timing is crucial in numerous contemporary situations. Whether it's launching a product, making an investment, or even sending an email, the right timing can make a significant difference in the outcome.

«Therefore, the good fighter will be terrible in his onset and prompt in his decision.» - Sun Tzu

Sun Tzu underlines the attributes of a good warrior: being formidable in attack and quick in decision-making.

[Translator's Note]

In a modern context, this could refer to the need for decisiveness and boldness in competitive situations, whether in business, sports, or other fields. It also emphasizes the value of swift decision-making, a critical skill in today's fast-paced world.

Sun Tzu's wisdom in Chapter 5, «Energy,» highlights the importance of timing and decisiveness, providing valuable lessons for readers in diverse contemporary contexts.

«Energy may be likened to the bending of a crossbow; decision, to the releasing of a trigger.» - Sun Tzu

Sun Tzu uses the metaphor of a crossbow to illustrate the concepts of energy and decision. He likens energy to the tension in a drawn crossbow and decision to the release of its trigger, emphasizing the importance of proper preparation and timely action.

[Translator's Note]

This analogy can be applied in various fields today. In business, for instance, energy could be likened to the preparation and planning that goes into a new project, while decision could be the point at which plans are set into motion.

«Amid the turmoil and tumult of battle, there may be seeming disorder and yet no real disorder at all; amid confusion and chaos, your array may be without head or tail, yet it will be proof against defeat.» - Sun Tzu

Sun Tzu suggests that even in the seeming disorder of battle, a well-led force maintains a deep-rooted order, and in spite of the apparent chaos, can remain undefeated.

[Translator's Note]

This insight could be understood in contemporary terms as the need for robust systems and structures that can withstand external disruptions. Despite the chaotic nature of, for example, the market, well-structured organizations can adapt and even thrive.

In this portion of Chapter 5, «Energy,» Sun Tzu uses engaging metaphors to present timeless wisdom on preparation, timely action, and the power of organization amidst chaos.

«Simulated disorder postulates perfect discipline; simulated fear postulates courage; simulated weakness postulates strength.»
- Sun Tzu

Sun Tzu notes that seeming disorder, fear, or weakness can be strategic simulations predicated on the existence of discipline, courage, and strength. This underscores the strategic use of deception in warfare.

[Translator's Note]

In modern contexts, these principles could be seen in businesses that underplay their strengths to lull competitors into complacency or governments that maintain a calm exterior despite internal challenges. It shows the importance of strategic appearances and the power of perception.

«Hiding order beneath the cloak of disorder is simply a question of subdivision; concealing courage under a show of timidity presupposes a fund of latent energy; masking strength with weakness is to be effected by tactical dispositions.» - Sun Tzu

Sun Tzu elaborates on how to create illusions of disorder, fear, and weakness: by careful subdivision, harnessing latent energy, and through tactical dispositions.

[Translator's Note]

This speaks to the need for strategic planning and tactical decision-making in any competitive situation. For instance, a business might intentionally launch a 'weak' product to distract competitors while it develops a more innovative solution.

Through this section of Chapter 5, «Energy», Sun Tzu offers valuable lessons on the strategic use of perception and deception, principles that remain relevant in numerous modern contexts.

«Thus one who is skillful at keeping the enemy on the move maintains deceitful appearances, according to which the enemy will act.» - Sun Tzu

Sun Tzu points out that a skillful strategist keeps the enemy guessing and reacting by maintaining deceitful appearances. It is a game of manipulation, with the strategist controlling the narrative.

[Translator's Note]

This principle is prevalent in various contemporary fields such as politics, business, and even sports. By manipulating perceptions, leaders can keep competitors on the back foot, reacting rather than acting proactively.

«He sacrifices something, that the enemy may snatch at it.» - Sun Tzu

Sun Tzu suggests the use of sacrifice as a means to lure the enemy, offering something appealing to provoke a desired response.

[Translator's Note]

This strategy is often seen in business, where a company may decide to make a sacrifice (like lowering prices) to lure customers away from competitors or to gain market share. It underscores the principle that sometimes, short-term losses can lead to long-term gains.

In these parts of Chapter 5, «Energy,» Sun Tzu presents the strategic use of manipulation and sacrifice, providing timeless wisdom that resonates with modern readers across diverse fields.

«By holding out baits, he keeps him on the march; then with a body of picked men he lies in wait for him.» - Sun Tzu

Sun Tzu describes a strategy of luring the enemy into a trap using bait, then waiting with a select group of troops to ambush them, emphasizing the power of deception and tactical planning.

[Translator's Note]

This could apply in many modern contexts, such as business or sports. A team might use a specific player or strategy as a 'bait' to distract the opposition, then surprise them with an unexpected maneuver.

«The clever combatant looks to the effect of combined energy and does not require too much from individuals.» - Sun Tzu

Sun Tzu advises that a wise warrior does not rely on the strength of individual soldiers but on the combined energy of the entire force, highlighting the importance of teamwork and synergy.

[Translator's Note]

In today's world, this principle can be applied to the importance of teamwork in any organization or venture. The combined efforts of a well-coordinated team often outweigh the capabilities of individual members, no matter how talented.

In these excerpts from Chapter 5, «Energy,» Sun Tzu illustrates the effectiveness of tactical deception and the power of collective action, providing valuable insights for readers in various contemporary scenarios.

«Hence his ability to pick out the right men and utilize combined energy.» - Sun Tzu

Sun Tzu points out that a wise leader not only selects the right individuals but also knows how to harness their collective energy, emphasizing the roles of discernment and coordination in leadership.

[Translator's Note]

In modern contexts, this could refer to the importance of talent acquisition and team management in an organization. Leaders who can identify the right people for a task and foster collaboration among them are often more successful.

«When he utilizes combined energy, his fighting men become as it were like rolling logs or stones.» - Sun Tzu

Here, Sun Tzu compares an army utilizing combined energy to rolling logs or stones - unstoppable and powerful, emphasizing the potential of unified action.

[Translator's Note]

In contemporary terms, this could be likened to the momentum generated by a cohesive team working towards a shared goal, whether in a business setting, a sports team, or any group-oriented endeavor.

These passages in Chapter 5, «Energy,» continue to showcase Sun Tzu's timeless wisdom on leadership and the power of collective action, offering profound insights for today's leaders across various fields.

«For it is the nature of a log or stone to remain motionless on level ground, and to move when on a slope; if four-cornered, to come to a standstill, but if round-shaped, to go rolling down.» - Sun Tzu

Sun Tzu uses the metaphor of logs and stones to explain that things behave according to their nature and circumstances. Just as logs and stones move or stay still depending on their shape and the terrain, individuals and groups behave differently based on their nature and environment.

[Translator's Note]

In a modern context, this could be seen as the importance of understanding the strengths, weaknesses, and unique qualities of team members, and also the impact of the environment on their performance. Effective leadership involves creating conditions that encourage the team to move towards the goal like a rolling stone.

«Thus the energy developed by good fighting men is as the momentum of a round stone rolled down a mountain thousands of feet in height.» - Sun Tzu

Here, Sun Tzu compares the energy of well-trained soldiers to a stone rolling down a mountain, gaining unstoppable momentum, underscoring the power of effective training and preparation.

[Translator's Note]

This principle holds true in any field today. Adequate preparation and training can create a momentum that becomes hard to stop, whether in a business launching a new product, an athlete preparing for a competition, or a team working on a project.

Chapter 5, «Energy,» continues to offer profound insights on understanding the nature of teams and the power of preparation, applicable in numerous contemporary situations.

«Therefore, the clever combatant imposes his will on the enemy but does not allow the enemy's will to be imposed on him.»
- Sun Tzu

Sun Tzu emphasizes the importance of controlling the dynamics of a conflict, illustrating that the successful strategist actively directs the battle but does not become reactionary to the enemy's moves.

[Translator's Note]

In today's context, this principle could apply to numerous areas, such as business or diplomacy. It speaks to the importance of maintaining proactive control in negotiations or competitive situations, rather than merely reacting to the moves of others.

«By holding out advantages to him, he can cause the enemy to approach of his own accord; or, by inflicting damage, he can make it impossible for the enemy to draw near.» - Sun Tzu

Sun Tzu discusses the strategic use of both incentives and threats to control the enemy's actions, showing how a masterful leader can manipulate situations to their advantage.

[Translator's Note]

This strategic approach remains relevant in contemporary fields like business or politics. Leaders can use incentives to attract partners or stakeholders, and deterrents to discourage undesirable actions or behaviors.

In this portion of Chapter 5, «Energy,» Sun Tzu explores how a strategic leader can control conflict dynamics, providing valuable lessons for readers navigating modern situations.

«If the enemy is taking his ease, he can harass him; if well supplied with food, he can starve him out; if quietly encamped, he can force him to move.» - Sun Tzu

Sun Tzu outlines how a strategist can disrupt the enemy's comfort, resources, and stability. It highlights the importance of not only understanding your enemy's current situation but also actively seeking to destabilize it.

[Translator's Note]

In the modern context, this could translate to identifying your competitor's comfort zones, resource strengths, and stability, and devising strategies to challenge them. For instance, a business could launch a rival product, undercut pricing, or disrupt market conditions to challenge a competitor.

«Appear at points which the enemy must hasten to defend; march swiftly to places where you are not expected.» - Sun Tzu

Sun Tzu suggests creating diversions and being unpredictable as a strategy, highlighting the effectiveness of surprising the enemy.

[Translator's Note]

In today's world, this strategy could be seen in how companies innovate unexpectedly or create diversions through marketing campaigns. It underscores the power of innovation, speed, and the element of surprise.

Through these parts of Chapter 5, «Energy,» Sun Tzu provides timeless wisdom on competition strategy that remains relevant for contemporary readers in various fields.

«An army may march great distances without distress if it marches through country where the enemy is not.» - Sun Tzu

Sun Tzu highlights the strategic advantage of avoiding direct confrontation with the enemy when possible. This advice emphasizes the importance of choosing the path of least resistance to conserve energy and resources.

[Translator's Note]

This insight remains applicable in today's business landscape, where companies often find success by entering unoccupied market segments or creating new ones, rather than directly competing with established entities.

«You can be sure of succeeding in your attacks if you only attack places which are undefended.» - Sun Tzu

Sun Tzu stresses the value of identifying and targeting the enemy's weak spots, an approach that increases the likelihood of success.

[Translator's Note]

This strategic principle can be seen in modern contexts such as businesses targeting a competitor's weaker product lines or exploiting gaps in their service offerings. It highlights the importance of careful competitor analysis and strategic planning.

In these excerpts from Chapter 5, «Energy,» Sun Tzu's timeless wisdom offers valuable lessons on strategic planning and execution, which are applicable to numerous fields in the contemporary world.

«You can ensure the safety of your defense if you only hold positions that cannot be attacked.» - Sun Tzu

Sun Tzu underlines the importance of positioning in defense, emphasizing that impenetrable locations ensure security.

[Translator's Note]

In a modern context, this might translate into the importance of creating a robust defensive strategy that leaves no room for breaches. This could apply to cybersecurity, where a system's safety is ensured by eliminating vulnerabilities, or to a business's market position, where defensibility is created by unique products or strong brand loyalty.

«Hence that general is skillful in attack whose opponent does not know what to defend; and he is skillful in defense whose opponent does not know what to attack.» - Sun Tzu

Sun Tzu highlights that the ability to keep one's strategies hidden from the opponent is a significant advantage, both in attack and defense.

[Translator's Note]

This principle is evident in numerous modern contexts, such as business, sports, or cybersecurity. The ability to keep strategies and vulnerabilities hidden can provide a significant advantage over competitors or opponents.

In these parts of Chapter 5, «Energy,» Sun Tzu emphasizes the importance of strategic positioning and the power of secrecy, providing timeless wisdom that resonates with readers in various contemporary scenarios.

«O divine art of subtlety and secrecy! Through you we learn to be invisible, through you inaudible; and hence we can hold the enemy's fate in our hands.» - Sun Tzu

Sun Tzu extols the virtues of subtlety and secrecy, suggesting they confer the power to control outcomes by remaining unseen and unheard, controlling the enemy's fate.

[Translator's Note]

In the contemporary world, the principle of discretion and subtlety holds relevance in various fields, including business strategy, negotiation tactics, or cybersecurity. By keeping plans and vulnerabilities hidden, one can gain a strategic advantage.

«You may advance and be absolutely irresistible if you make for the enemy's weak points; you may retire and be safe from pursuit if your movements are more rapid than those of the enemy.» - Sun Tzu

Sun Tzu outlines a twofold strategy: attacking the enemy's weaknesses makes you unstoppable, and faster movements ensure safety during retreat. It emphasizes the importance of speed and the identification of vulnerabilities.

[Translator's Note]

This principle could apply to various modern scenarios, from competitive business strategy to sports. Fast, agile maneuvers combined with a focus on the competitor's weaknesses often yield successful results.

In these parts of Chapter 5, «Energy,» Sun Tzu showcases the strategic advantages of subtlety, speed, and a focus on vulnerabilities, providing valuable insights for readers across diverse fields.

«If we wish to fight, the enemy can be forced to an engagement even though he be sheltered behind a high rampart and a deep ditch. All we need do is attack some other place that he will be obliged to relieve.» - Sun Tzu

Sun Tzu suggests a strategy of distraction to draw the enemy out of a secure position. By attacking a secondary location, the enemy is compelled to react, creating an opportunity for engagement.

[Translator's Note]

This tactic could be employed in a modern business context, where launching a new product or initiative could force a competitor to respond, diverting their focus from their primary objectives. This is an example of a feint or diversionary strategy.

«If we do not wish to fight, we can prevent the enemy from engaging us even though the lines of our encampment be merely traced out on the ground. All we need do is to throw something odd and unaccountable in his way.» - Sun Tzu

Sun Tzu illustrates how creating confusion can be used as a defensive tactic to avoid engagement with the enemy. By introducing an unexpected element, the enemy's advance can be halted.

[Translator's Note]

In a modern context, this could be viewed as a company introducing an unconventional product or strategy to confuse competitors and prevent direct competition. It highlights the value of unpredictability as a defensive strategy.

These excerpts from Chapter 5, «Energy,» delve into the strategic use of distraction and confusion in both offensive and defensive situations, offering useful insights for various contemporary scenarios.

«By discovering the enemy's dispositions and remaining invisible ourselves, we can keep our forces concentrated, while the enemy's must be divided.» - Sun Tzu

Sun Tzu stresses the importance of information and invisibility. By knowing the enemy's positions and plans, while keeping your own hidden, you can maintain a concentrated force, forcing the enemy to divide theirs in response to unseen threats.

[Translator's Note]

In modern business, sports, or warfare, the principle of gathering intelligence on competitors while concealing your strategies remains key. It ensures the efficient use of resources and often leads to a strategic advantage.

«We can form a single united body, while the enemy must split up into fractions. Hence there will be a whole pitted against separate parts of a whole, which means that we shall be many to the enemy's few.» - Sun Tzu

Sun Tzu points out that by forcing the enemy to divide their forces in response to threats, you can confront separate, weaker factions with your united strength. This is a tactic of divide and conquer.

[Translator's Note]

This strategy remains relevant in a variety of contexts, from business to politics, where forcing competitors or opponents to spread their resources thin across multiple fronts can allow for a more concentrated and effective effort on your part.

Through these parts of Chapter 5, «Energy,» Sun Tzu offers valuable insight on the advantages of information, invisibility, and division, all of which remain relevant strategies in numerous modern fields.

«And if we are able thus to attack an inferior force with a superior one, our opponents will be in dire straits.» - Sun Tzu

Sun Tzu emphasizes the advantage of pitting a superior force against a weaker one, suggesting that such a situation puts the enemy in a dire position.

[Translator's Note]

This principle is visible in today's contexts such as business competition or sporting events. A team or organization with superior resources, talent, or strategy can often overwhelm a less equipped opponent, leading to a significant advantage.

«The spot where we intend to fight must not be made known; for then the enemy will have to prepare against a possible attack at several different points.» - Sun Tzu

Sun Tzu advises keeping battle plans secret, making the enemy prepare for multiple potential attacks, and consequently spreading their defenses thin.

[Translator's Note]

In modern times, this strategy applies to any competitive situation, including business, politics, or sports. By keeping strategies confidential, one can prevent opponents from preparing effectively, thereby gaining an advantage.

In these parts of Chapter 5, «Energy,» Sun Tzu focuses on the strength of superior forces and the power of secrecy, offering strategic insights applicable in various contemporary scenarios.

«And the numbers of the enemy that we capture will be the reward of our victory.» - Sun Tzu

Sun Tzu suggests that the number of enemies captured is a tangible measure of victory, implying that in warfare, success isn't just about surviving, but also about diminishing the opponent's capacity to fight.

[Translator's Note]

In a modern context, this could be interpreted as a call to not only achieve success in one's endeavors, but also to outperform competitors. This could apply to business, sports, or any competitive environment.

«But if in the midst of difficulties we are always ready to seize an advantage, we may extricate ourselves from misfortune.» - Sun Tzu

Sun Tzu advises that even in the face of adversity, being alert to opportunities can lead to a reversal of fortune. This wisdom underscores the value of resilience and strategic thinking.

[Translator's Note]

This principle is applicable in today's world where resilience and adaptability are often key to overcoming challenges in various fields, from business and politics to personal development.

In these portions of Chapter 5, «Energy,» Sun Tzu emphasizes the importance of strategic advantage in both offensive and defensive situations, offering insights that remain valuable in a range of contemporary scenarios.

«Reduce the hostile chiefs by inflicting damage on them; and make trouble for them, and keep them constantly engaged; hold out specious allurements, and make them rush to any given point.» - Sun Tzu

Sun Tzu recommends a strategy of disruption, advising to keep the enemy constantly engaged and distracted with alluring deceptions. This strategy emphasizes the importance of keeping the enemy off balance and in a reactive state.

[Translator's Note]

This strategy could be seen in a modern business context, where companies might employ disruption tactics to distract competitors, forcing them to divert resources and attention away from their main objectives. This can also apply to political campaigns, where keeping an opponent constantly engaged can give an advantage.

«The art of war teaches us to rely not on the likelihood of the enemy's not coming, but on our own readiness to receive him; not on the chance of his not attacking, but rather on the fact that we have made our position unassailable.» - Sun Tzu

Sun Tzu advises against reliance on the enemy's inaction and instead advocates preparedness and creating an unassailable position. This reflects the essence of the defensive strategy - not hoping the enemy won't attack, but being ready when they do.

[Translator's Note]

This strategic insight is relevant in modern contexts like business, where a company's strength lies not in hoping competitors won't challenge them, but in building robust products, services, or strategies that can withstand such challenges.

Through these excerpts from Chapter 5, «Energy,» Sun Tzu continues to provide valuable insights into offensive and defensive strategies, which are applicable to various fields in the modern world.

«There are five dangerous faults which may affect a general: (1) Recklessness, which leads to destruction; (2) cowardice, which leads to capture; (3) a hasty temper, which can be provoked by insults; (4) a delicacy of honor which is sensitive to shame; (5) over-solicitude for his men, which exposes him to worry and trouble.» - Sun Tzu

Sun Tzu lists five dangerous traits that can lead a general to failure: recklessness, cowardice, hastiness, excessive honor, and over-concern for his troops. Each of these characteristics, when in excess, can be detrimental to leadership and the overall success of a campaign.

[Translator's Note]

These traits remain relevant in modern contexts as potential pitfalls for leaders in various fields. Overconfidence can lead to uncalculated risks, while excessive caution can cause missed opportunities. Hastiness can lead to rushed decisions, while being overly sensitive to shame may prevent necessary actions. Lastly, excessive concern can result in overprotectiveness, hampering the team's growth and progress.

Through these concluding parts of Chapter 5, «Energy,» Sun Tzu offers timeless wisdom about the qualities of successful leadership, providing valuable lessons that apply well beyond the battlefield and into the realms of modern-day leadership, management, and personal development.

Chapter 6: Weak Points and Strong

«Sun Tzu said: Whoever is first in the field and awaits the coming of the enemy, will be fresh for the fight; whoever is second in the field and has to hasten to battle will arrive exhausted.» - Sun Tzu

Sun Tzu emphasizes the advantages of anticipation and preparation in warfare. The side that positions itself first and waits for the enemy will be rested and ready, whereas the side that arrives later will be tired and less prepared.

[Translator's Note]

In the modern world, this principle can be applied to many areas such as business, academics, sports, and more. Those who prepare early and anticipate challenges often have an advantage over those who react and rush to meet the same challenges.

«Therefore, the clever combatant imposes his will on the enemy but does not allow the enemy's will to be imposed on him.»
- Sun Tzu

Sun Tzu advises the strategist to control the battlefield by imposing their will on the enemy and refusing to be dominated by the enemy's intentions. This advice underscores the importance of initiative and control in any conflict situation.

[Translator's Note]

In a contemporary setting, this could mean setting the terms of a business negotiation, controlling the pace of a sports match, or shaping public discourse in a political campaign. The party that sets the terms often has the upper hand.

The opening sections of Chapter 6, «Weak Points and Strong,» provide key insights into the power of preparation and initiative, lessons that continue to resonate in many areas of modern life.

«By holding out advantages to him, he can cause the enemy to approach of his own accord; or, by inflicting damage, he can make it impossible for the enemy to draw near.» - Sun Tzu

Sun Tzu describes the power of incentives and threats in warfare. By offering benefits, the enemy can be lured into a trap, while by causing harm, the enemy can be kept at bay. This reflects the strategic use of both the carrot and the stick.

[Translator's Note]

This strategy can be seen in many contemporary situations. For example, in business, a company can lure customers from competitors by offering superior benefits. Alternatively, a company can prevent competition by creating barriers to entry or maintaining a high standard of service or product quality.

«If the enemy is taking his ease, he can harass him; if well supplied with food, he can starve him out; if quietly encamped, he can force him to move.» - Sun Tzu

Sun Tzu provides a series of strategic actions designed to disrupt the enemy's comfort and stability. His approach involves directly opposing the enemy's current state to create imbalance and discomfort.

[Translator's Note]

In a modern context, these tactics could be employed in a business setting to unsettle competitors. For example, a disruptive innovation could «harass» an established market leader, a price war could «starve out» a well-resourced competitor, or a new regulatory challenge could force a «quietly encamped» competitor to change its strategy.

Through these portions of Chapter 6, «Weak Points and Strong,» Sun Tzu further extends his discourse on strategy and manipulation, delivering insights that can be employed in a variety of modern scenarios.

«Appear at points which the enemy must hasten to defend; march swiftly to places where you are not expected.» - Sun Tzu

Sun Tzu advocates for unpredictability and agility. By appearing where the enemy feels compelled to defend, you force them into a reactive stance. Furthermore, by moving quickly to unexpected places, you retain the element of surprise.

[Translator's Note]

In modern contexts, such as in business or sports, this strategy of unpredictability and speed can provide a competitive edge. For example, businesses can surprise competitors by entering new markets unexpectedly or launching innovative products without warning.

«An army may march great distances without distress if it marches through country where the enemy is not.» - Sun Tzu

Sun Tzu notes the advantage of moving through unopposed territory. It conserves energy and reduces the risk of conflict, allowing for greater mobility and speed.

[Translator's Note]

In modern business, this could represent the advantage of pioneering into unoccupied market spaces or niches, which often involve fewer competitive pressures and lower resource expenditure for potentially higher returns.

In these parts of Chapter 6, «Weak Points and Strong,» Sun Tzu offers valuable insight on the benefits of unpredictability, speed, and choosing the path of least resistance, concepts that remain highly applicable in numerous modern fields.

«You can be sure of succeeding in your attacks if you only attack places which are undefended. You can ensure the safety of your defense if you only hold positions that cannot be attacked.» - Sun Tzu

Sun Tzu emphasizes the strategy of attacking undefended places and holding positions that cannot be attacked. This minimizes the risk of failure in attack and ensures the safety of defense, portraying the importance of choosing battles wisely.

[Translator's Note]

In the modern world, this might translate into focusing on market areas where competition is minimal or establishing a business model that is hard for competitors to replicate. It represents the principle of seeking advantage while minimizing risk.

«Hence that general is skillful in attack whose opponent does not know what to defend; and he is skillful in defense whose opponent does not know what to attack.» - Sun Tzu

Sun Tzu outlines the advantage of unpredictability in both offense and defense. If the enemy is unsure about what to defend or attack, it gives a significant advantage to the unpredictable party.

[Translator's Note]

This concept can be applied in modern competitive situations like business or sports, where keeping one's strategies and tactics unpredictable can lead to significant advantages.

Through these sections of Chapter 6, «Weak Points and Strong,» Sun Tzu continues to provide strategic wisdom that stands the test of time, offering insights relevant to modern fields such as business, politics, and more.

«O divine art of subtlety and secrecy! Through you we learn to be invisible, through you inaudible; and hence we can hold the enemy's fate in our hands.» - Sun Tzu

Sun Tzu praises the virtues of subtlety and secrecy in warfare, suggesting that they grant an army the ability to control its enemy's fate. This underscores the importance of information control and stealth in any conflict.

[Translator's Note]

In today's world, the principles of subtlety and secrecy can be applied in various fields such as business, where competitive advantages often rely on proprietary knowledge, stealthy product development, or discreet negotiation strategies.

«You may advance and be absolutely irresistible if you make for the enemy's weak points; you may retire and be safe from pursuit if your movements are more rapid than those of the enemy.» - Sun Tzu

Sun Tzu asserts that focusing on the enemy's weak points can lead to overwhelming success, and rapid movements can ensure safe retreats. Speed and targeting weaknesses are both strategic elements that can tilt the balance in one's favor.

[Translator's Note]

In a modern context, businesses often gain the upper hand by identifying and exploiting competitors' weaknesses or by moving quickly to adapt to market changes. Similarly, rapid responses to crises can mitigate potential damages.

In the concluding parts of Chapter 6, «Weak Points and Strong,» Sun Tzu's wisdom shines through, providing timeless insights into strategy, speed, and the power of subtlety - principles that continue to have a profound impact in a wide range of contemporary fields.

Chapter 7: Maneuvering

«Sun Tzu said: In war, the general receives his commands from the sovereign, collects his army and concentrates his forces.» - Sun Tzu

Sun Tzu introduces the chapter by outlining the hierarchical structure of command in warfare and the importance of assembling and focusing forces. This underlines the essential roles of authority, organization, and concentration in any strategic undertaking.

[Translator's Note]

In today's corporate or organizational environment, the principle remains the same. Decisions often flow from the top (board of directors, CEO) to the management team, who are then responsible for marshalling resources and focusing efforts to achieve strategic objectives.

«When you leave your own country behind and take your army across neighborhood territory, you find yourself on critical ground. When there are means of communication on all four sides, the ground is one of intersecting highways.» - Sun Tzu

Sun Tzu highlights the strategic implications of different terrains. Venturing far from home turf and into intersecting highways implies a precarious situation, suggesting the necessity to adapt strategies based on geographical and situational realities.

[Translator's Note]

In a modern business context, this might mean navigating unfamiliar markets or regulatory landscapes, signifying the importance of understanding and adapting to different environments and conditions.

In the opening sections of Chapter 7, «Maneuvering,» Sun Tzu sets the stage for an exploration of the complex dynamics of strategy and environment, laying the groundwork for insights that remain relevant in various modern arenas.

«When you penetrate deeply into a country, it is serious ground. When you penetrate a little way, it is facile ground.» - Sun Tzu

Sun Tzu highlights how the degree of penetration into enemy territory affects the seriousness of the situation. Deep penetration indicates a serious commitment and potentially greater risks, while shallow penetration represents a less risky, more easily reversible situation.

[Translator's Note]

This concept is applicable in modern-day scenarios like business expansion. Deep penetration into new markets or product lines signifies a significant investment and risk, while a shallower, more tentative approach carries less risk and commitment.

«When you have the enemy's strongholds on your rear, and narrow passes in front, it is hemmed-in ground. When there is no place of refuge at all, it is desperate ground.» - Sun Tzu

Sun Tzu describes various types of challenging terrain and the corresponding strategic implications. When hemmed in or on desperate ground, the options are limited and the situation is dangerous, urging an army to fight with greater determination.

[Translator's Note]

In contemporary contexts, this might be compared to a business facing severe competitive pressures or even a potential bankruptcy, prompting it to innovate, pivot, or fight harder to survive.

Continuing through Chapter 7, «Maneuvering,» Sun Tzu provides insights on situational analysis and response, offering wisdom that can be translated into a variety of contemporary settings, from business strategy to crisis management.

«Therefore, on dispersive ground, I would inspire my men with unity of purpose. On facile ground, I would see that there is close connection between all parts of my army.» - Sun Tzu

On dispersive ground, where an army might be tempted to disperse, Sun Tzu highlights the importance of instilling unity of purpose. On facile ground, where the situation is less serious, he stresses the need for coordination among all parts of the army.

[Translator's Note]

In a contemporary context, such as a business organization, these principles might translate into maintaining a clear company mission to keep employees engaged during challenging times and ensuring good communication and collaboration across departments during times of relative calm.

«On contentious ground, I would hurry up my rear. On open ground, I would keep a vigilant eye on my defenses. On ground of intersecting highways, I would consolidate my alliances.» - Sun Tzu

Sun Tzu offers specific strategies for different types of ground. On contentious ground, it's essential to move quickly; on open ground, defenses must be maintained; on ground of intersecting highways, alliances become crucial.

[Translator's Note]

These insights could be reflected in modern scenarios where, for example, a business may need to quickly address emerging market challenges (contentious ground), ensure its cybersecurity is robust (open ground), or strengthen its partnerships in a competitive marketplace (intersecting highways).

In these parts of Chapter 7, «Maneuvering,» Sun Tzu elaborates on his nuanced understanding of terrain and situation, and how they inform strategic decisions – insights that find echoes in numerous contemporary scenarios.

«On serious ground, I would try to ensure a continuous stream of supplies. On difficult ground, I would keep pushing on along the road.» - Sun Tzu

Sun Tzu illustrates the importance of logistics and perseverance in challenging scenarios. Ensuring a steady supply chain in serious situations, and persistence in navigating difficult terrains, are strategies he advocates for.

[Translator's Note]

In modern contexts, like a challenging business environment, these strategies may translate into securing a reliable supply chain during crucial growth phases, or persevering through challenges to maintain momentum and progress.

«On hemmed-in ground, I would block any way of retreat. On desperate ground, I would proclaim to my soldiers the hopelessness of saving their lives.» - Sun Tzu

In extremely challenging situations, Sun Tzu recommends removing the option of retreat to force the troops to fight with their utmost effort. On desperate ground, he suggests that it might even be beneficial to make the soldiers aware of the dire situation to spur them into fighting with everything they have.

[Translator's Note]

While the exact application might not translate to a contemporary setting, the underlying principle of committing fully to a course of action in certain situations still holds. For example, in a business facing a crisis, transparency about the severity of the situation can rally the team to give their best effort to overcome the difficulties.

With these passages from Chapter 7, «Maneuvering,» Sun Tzu imparts invaluable wisdom on dealing with different types of challenges, providing principles that remain applicable in many modern-day scenarios.

«For it is the soldier's disposition to offer an obstinate resistance when surrounded, to fight hard when he cannot help himself, and to obey promptly when he has fallen into danger.» - Sun Tzu

Sun Tzu identifies the inherent nature of soldiers to resist when surrounded, fight when cornered, and obey when in danger. This suggests the importance of understanding and utilizing the natural dispositions of one's team in any strategic situation.

[Translator's Note]

In modern contexts, this insight can be valuable for leaders in any organization. By understanding their team's tendencies under pressure, they can better manage crises and lead their teams effectively.

«We cannot enter into alliances until we are acquainted with the designs of our neighbors.» - Sun Tzu

Sun Tzu advises caution and knowledge before entering alliances, reinforcing the critical importance of understanding others' intentions and strategies.

[Translator's Note]

This concept remains highly relevant in today's world, where businesses, countries, and individuals form alliances. Understanding the motivations, strengths, and intentions of potential partners is essential before entering into any cooperative agreement.

In these concluding sections of Chapter 7, «Maneuvering,» Sun Tzu underscores the importance of understanding one's team and allies, offering timeless wisdom that continues to inform effective leadership and partnership strategies in contemporary times.

Chapter 8: The Nine Situations

«Sun Tzu said: The art of war recognizes nine varieties of ground.» - Sun Tzu

Sun Tzu begins this chapter by introducing the concept of nine varieties of ground, each with its strategic implications. These varieties, he suggests, offer different challenges and opportunities in warfare.

[Translator's Note]

In modern contexts, such as business, these varieties of ground might represent different market conditions or business environments, each requiring its unique approach or strategy.

«When a chieftain is fighting in his own territory, it is dispersive ground.» - Sun Tzu

Sun Tzu's first variety of ground is 'dispersive ground,' which refers to fighting on home territory. This situation may offer certain advantages but can also lead to complacency or lack of unity.

[Translator's Note]

In a business context, 'dispersive ground' might equate to operating in a familiar or domestic market. While this may provide advantages like knowledge of local conditions, there might be risks, such as taking things for granted or failing to innovate due to familiarity.

In these opening sections of Chapter 8, «The Nine Situations,» Sun Tzu begins to outline his classification of different types of ground, offering key insights that remain adaptable to a wide range of modern strategic scenarios.

«When he has penetrated into hostile territory, but to no great distance, it is facile ground.» - Sun Tzu

The second type of ground that Sun Tzu describes is 'facile ground.' This refers to territory that has been entered but not deeply penetrated. The situation presents its own challenges and opportunities.

[Translator's Note]

In today's business context, 'facile ground' might refer to initial market entry or pilot project implementation. While it presents an opportunity to test and learn, the shallow commitment may also mean fewer resources or lower priority compared to more established operations.

«Ground the possession of which imports great advantage to either side, is contentious ground.» - Sun Tzu

'Contentious ground' is the third type of ground described by Sun Tzu. This refers to terrain that offers significant strategic advantage to whoever controls it, making it a subject of contention.

[Translator's Note]

In the contemporary business landscape, 'contentious ground' could symbolize a high-value market segment or a key technological advantage. These resources are often contested fiercely by competitors due to their potential for high returns.

In these sections of Chapter 8, «The Nine Situations,» Sun Tzu further elaborates on his classification of different types of ground, providing frameworks that can be translated into various modern settings, from business strategy to geopolitical analysis.

«Ground on which each side has liberty of movement is open ground.» - Sun Tzu

The fourth type of ground that Sun Tzu introduces is 'open ground.' This refers to terrain where both sides can move freely, a situation that may require caution and careful strategic planning.

[Translator's Note]

In contemporary contexts, 'open ground' could refer to a deregulated market or an emerging industry where there is a high level of freedom for all players to operate. This environment requires strategic foresight and a proactive approach to navigate effectively.

«Ground which forms the key to three contiguous states, so that he who occupies it first has most of the Empire at his command, is a ground of intersecting highways.» - Sun Tzu

The fifth type of ground, 'ground of intersecting highways,' refers to a strategically important location that commands access to multiple areas. Its occupation confers significant advantage.

[Translator's Note]

In a modern business environment, 'ground of intersecting highways' could represent a strategic position that allows control over various market segments or supply chains. Securing such a position could provide a competitive advantage and extensive market influence.

In these parts of Chapter 8, «The Nine Situations,» Sun Tzu continues to delve into the strategic implications of different types of ground, offering timeless insights that resonate in a variety of contemporary scenarios.

«Ground which can be abandoned but is hard to re-occupy is called entangling.» - Sun Tzu

The sixth type of ground Sun Tzu describes is 'entangling ground.' This refers to terrain that, once abandoned, becomes difficult to re-occupy. It suggests a careful consideration of strategic moves, as reversing them could be challenging.

[Translator's Note]

In a modern business context, 'entangling ground' might refer to a market segment or business model that, once left, could be difficult to re-enter due to factors such as competition, changing customer preferences, or regulatory changes.

«From a position of this sort, if the enemy is unprepared, you may sally forth and defeat him. But if the enemy is prepared for your coming, and you fail to defeat him, then, return being impossible, disaster will ensue.» - Sun Tzu

Sun Tzu highlights the risks and opportunities associated with 'entangling ground.' If an enemy is unprepared, an advantage can be seized; however, if the enemy is prepared and not defeated, retreat may not be an option, leading to potential disaster.

[Translator's Note]

This lesson could be applied to business scenarios where a company decides to venture into a highly competitive market segment. If the competition is unprepared, the company might gain an advantage. However, if the competition is ready and the company fails to establish itself, it might find it difficult to retreat and refocus its resources, leading to significant losses.

Through these passages in Chapter 8, «The Nine Situations,» Sun Tzu further elaborates on the complexity of different types of ground, offering valuable strategic insights for various contexts..

«When the position is such that neither side will gain by making the first move, it is called temporizing ground.» - Sun Tzu

The seventh type of ground that Sun Tzu introduces is 'temporizing ground.' This refers to a situation where neither party stands to gain significantly from initiating action. It suggests a strategic stalemate where patience and waiting for the right opportunity may be the best approach.

[Translator's Note]

In modern terms, 'temporizing ground' could represent a saturated market where aggressive moves might not yield significant advantages, or where the costs of such moves outweigh potential benefits. In these situations, a company might find it more beneficial to bide its time and wait for the right opportunity.

«Ground which is reached through narrow gorges, and from which we can only retire by tortuous paths, so that a small number of the enemy would suffice to crush a large body of our men: this is hemmed in ground.» - Sun Tzu

Sun Tzu's eighth type of ground is 'hemmed in ground.' This refers to a terrain where movement is restricted due to natural features like narrow gorges. Such ground poses significant challenges due to its limitations on retreat and the advantage it provides to smaller forces.

[Translator's Note]

In contemporary contexts, 'hemmed in ground' might represent a restrictive regulatory environment or a niche market with limited growth opportunities. These scenarios require careful planning and strategy due to their inherent limitations and challenges.

In these sections of Chapter 8, «The Nine Situations,» Sun Tzu provides more insights into his classification of different types of ground, offering strategic wisdom that can be applied to a wide range of modern contexts.

«Ground on which we can only be saved from destruction by fighting without delay, is desperate ground.» - Sun Tzu

The ninth and final type of ground that Sun Tzu discusses is 'desperate ground.' This refers to a situation where immediate and decisive action is the only way to avoid disaster. It calls for boldness and commitment in the face of adversity.

[Translator's Note]

In today's world, 'desperate ground' might represent a business in crisis, such as facing imminent bankruptcy. In such situations, immediate, decisive, and often radical action may be the only way to save the company. This might include drastic cost-cutting, rapid innovation, or a significant strategic pivot.

«On desperate ground, fight.» - Sun Tzu

In the face of 'desperate ground,' Sun Tzu's advice is simple and direct: fight. This encapsulates the spirit of resilience and courage that is required when facing dire circumstances.

[Translator's Note]

This advice remains as relevant today as when it was first written. Whether in business, personal life, or any challenging situation, when there are no other options left, the only choice is to face the challenge head-on and fight.

In these concluding sections of Chapter 8, «The Nine Situations,» Sun Tzu finalizes his classification of different types of ground, culminating in a powerful call for courage and determination in the face of extreme challenges.

Chapter 9: The Army on the March

«Sun Tzu said: We come now to the question of encamping the army, and observing signs of the enemy.» - Sun Tzu

In the opening of this chapter, Sun Tzu moves the discussion from the analysis of different types of ground to practical considerations of encamping the army and understanding enemy signs.

[Translator's Note]

In a modern context, the concept of 'encamping the army' might translate to setting up operations or establishing a presence in a new market, while 'observing signs of the enemy' could refer to monitoring competitive activities, market trends, or customer behaviors.

«Pass quickly over mountains, and keep in the neighborhood of valleys.» - Sun Tzu

Sun Tzu advises swift passage over mountains, indicative of overcoming major obstacles swiftly to avoid prolonged exposure to risk. Meanwhile, he suggests staying near valleys, perhaps indicating the need to stay close to resources or areas of potential support.

[Translator's Note]

Translated to contemporary situations, this could mean overcoming challenges quickly and staying close to your resources - be it financial, human, or otherwise. Swift resolution of problems prevents them from escalating, and having easy access to resources helps to manage situations effectively.

As we enter Chapter 9, «The Army on the March,» Sun Tzu transitions from theoretical stratagems to more practical aspects of war, the principles of which continue to be applicable in various modern contexts.

«Camp in high places, facing the sun. Do not climb heights in order to fight.» - Sun Tzu

Sun Tzu advises to camp in high places with a clear view of surroundings and exposure to the sun, suggesting a strategic preference for clarity, oversight, and favorable conditions. However, he warns against climbing heights to fight, which might expose one's forces to unnecessary risk and exhaustion.

[Translator's Note]

In a modern context, this guidance could apply to businesses selecting their market positioning. Being in a 'high place' could symbolize a market leader position with clear oversight of the industry landscape. Yet, 'climbing heights to fight' might represent costly price wars or aggressive market competition that can drain resources and might not necessarily lead to a sustainable advantage.

«After crossing a river, you should get far away from it.» - Sun Tzu

The advice to distance oneself from a river after crossing it suggests the importance of not allowing past challenges to continue to pose a threat or distraction.

[Translator's Note]

In today's business world, this might translate into the idea of not lingering on past failures or challenges but instead moving forward towards new goals and opportunities. It's important to learn from past experiences but not to let them hold back progress.

Continuing with Chapter 9, «The Army on the March,» Sun Tzu provides practical advice on navigating the physical and strategic landscape of conflict. These insights, translated into modern terms, offer valuable lessons for decision-making and strategy in a variety of contexts..

«When you come to a hill or a bank, occupy the sunny side, with the slope on your right rear. Thus you will at once act for the benefit of your soldiers and utilize the natural advantages of the ground.» - Sun Tzu

Sun Tzu advises choosing locations with natural advantages and considering the wellbeing of your soldiers. This demonstrates his emphasis on combining tactical thinking with consideration for the troops' morale and health.

[Translator's Note]

Applied to a modern business scenario, this might suggest the importance of selecting advantageous market positions while also considering the well-being of your employees. Balancing strategic decision-making with fostering a positive work environment can lead to higher productivity and increased loyalty among staff.

«When, in consequence of heavy rains up-country, a river which you wish to ford is swollen and flecked with foam, you must wait until it subsides.» - Sun Tzu

Here, Sun Tzu highlights the importance of patience and adaptability in the face of unforeseen challenges, advising against hastily attempting to overcome obstacles when conditions are unfavorable.

[Translator's Note]

In a business context, this lesson underscores the importance of patience and timing in decision-making. For example, in a volatile market, it might be wise to wait for conditions to stabilize before making significant investments or changes in strategy.

In these sections of Chapter 9, «The Army on the March,» Sun Tzu continues to weave practical military advice with broader strategic principles, offering timeless wisdom that resonates in a variety of modern situations.

«Country in which there are precipitous cliffs with torrents running between, deep natural hollows, confined places, tangled thickets, quagmires and crevasses, should be left with all possible speed and not approached.» - Sun Tzu

Sun Tzu advises against approaching difficult terrain fraught with natural dangers, emphasizing the importance of recognizing and avoiding unnecessary risks in strategic planning.

[Translator's Note]

In the contemporary business landscape, this could represent avoiding markets or business decisions fraught with uncertainty, complex regulations, or intense competition. The underlying lesson is to thoroughly evaluate the risks and challenges associated with a decision and avoid those with unfavorable odds.

«While we keep away from such places, we should get the enemy to approach them; while we face them, we should let the enemy have them on his rear.» - Sun Tzu

Sun Tzu's strategy is not only to avoid such difficult situations himself but also to manipulate circumstances so that his enemy finds themselves in these precarious positions, demonstrating an understanding of how to use environmental conditions to one's advantage.

[Translator's Note]

This could translate to a business strategy where a company not only avoids high-risk markets or decisions but also maneuvers its competitors into these challenging situations. For instance, a company might introduce disruptive products or services that force competitors to respond in high-risk ways.

In these passages from Chapter 9, «The Army on the March,» Sun Tzu's wisdom, translated into modern contexts, continues to provide valuable insights for strategic decision-making, risk management, and competitive positioning.

«If in the neighborhood of your camp there should be any hilly country, ponds surrounded by aquatic grass, hollow basins filled with reeds, or woods with thick undergrowth, they must be carefully searched; for these are places where men in ambush or insidious spies are likely to be lurking.» - Sun Tzu

Sun Tzu brings attention to the hidden dangers that can lurk in seemingly harmless places, reminding his readers of the importance of vigilance and thorough inspection in ensuring safety and preventing unexpected attacks.

[Translator's Note]

In modern business contexts, this could be interpreted as a reminder to thoroughly research and understand all aspects of a business environment. Hidden dangers might lurk in overlooked details, like small market trends that could become significant, potential regulatory changes, or emerging competitors.

«When the enemy is close at hand and remains quiet, he is relying on the natural strength of his position. When he keeps aloof and tries to provoke a battle, he is anxious for the other side to advance.» - Sun Tzu

Sun Tzu provides a nuanced understanding of the enemy's behavior, teaching that silence and distance can indicate different strategies and intentions. This understanding aids in anticipating and responding effectively to the enemy's tactics.

[Translator's Note]

This wisdom can be applied in modern scenarios where understanding competitor behavior is crucial. For instance, a quiet competitor might be developing a strong product, while a competitor who is actively provoking may be looking to draw you into a costly battle.

In these sections of Chapter 9, «The Army on the March,» Sun Tzu presents the importance of thorough investigation and understanding of both the physical and competitive landscapes, offering valuable lessons applicable to strategic decisions in today's dynamic environments.

«If his place of encampment is easy of access, he is tendering a bait.» - Sun Tzu

Sun Tzu warns that if an enemy's encampment appears easily accessible, it may be a trap. He teaches the importance of skepticism and caution when things seem too easy or convenient.

[Translator's Note]

In a modern context, a business opportunity that seems too good to be true may indeed be a 'bait'. It's essential to undertake due diligence and assess the risks before jumping on such opportunities to avoid potential traps.

«Movement amongst the trees of a forest shows that the enemy is advancing. The appearance of a number of screens in the midst of thick grass means that the enemy wants to make us suspicious.» - Sun Tzu

Sun Tzu advises on signs to look out for when predicting an enemy's movements, highlighting the importance of discerning between genuine actions and attempts at deception.

[Translator's Note]

This speaks to the importance in today's business world of monitoring market movements and understanding competitor behavior. Not all moves indicate real threat, and some might be intended to distract or mislead. It's crucial to distinguish between actual strategic shifts and diversionary tactics.

Further into Chapter 9, «The Army on the March,» Sun Tzu's wisdom, when adapted to modern contexts, provides insightful guidance on caution, skepticism, and the interpretation of competitor behavior in strategic decision-making..

«The rising of birds in their flight is the sign of an ambuscade. Startled beasts indicate that a sudden attack is coming.» - Sun Tzu

Sun Tzu introduces the idea of paying attention to the environment for signs of impending danger. Changes in the behavior of animals can signal the enemy's movements, demonstrating the importance of awareness and observation.

[Translator's Note]

In a business context, this could translate to observing subtle changes in the market or industry that might signal shifts in customer behavior, emerging trends, or movements from competitors. Being attuned to these 'signals' can provide an early warning system to anticipate and prepare for change.

«When there is dust rising in a high column, it is the sign of chariots advancing; when the dust is low, but spread over a wide area, it betokens the approach of infantry. When it branches out in different directions, it shows that parties have been sent to collect firewood.» - Sun Tzu

Sun Tzu continues to emphasize the importance of awareness and observation, this time demonstrating how to interpret different signals. These details can provide vital information about the enemy's activities and movements.

[Translator's Note]

This wisdom applies to business by reminding leaders to be attentive to various 'signs' in the market, such as changes in customer preferences, shifts in market trends, or activities of competitors. Different 'signals' can indicate different actions, and interpreting them correctly can provide strategic advantage.

As we delve further into Chapter 9, «The Army on the March,» Sun Tzu's teachings, translated to modern contexts, provide valuable lessons in observation, interpretation, and anticipatory action, all of which remain crucial in navigating today's complex and dynamic business environments.

«A few men, appearing to be in haste and flurried, are the decoy to some stratagem.» - Sun Tzu

Sun Tzu warns of the potential for deception in enemy tactics, reminding his readers to be wary of seemingly chaotic or hasty behavior, which could be a smokescreen for a more calculated plan.

[Translator's Note]

In modern business situations, this might be a reminder not to underestimate a competitor who appears disorganized or chaotic. This could be a distraction tactic masking a more strategic move. As such, businesses should maintain vigilance and conduct thorough analysis before reacting to competitors' actions.

«Humidity at the upper end and dryness at the lower end of a river; the moon's having left its usual position and gone to the other side, and the stars not being in their places; the appearance of double halos around the sun or moon, and the sounding of earth shocks; all these are omens of the coming of wind and rain.» - Sun Tzu

Sun Tzu shares his knowledge of natural signs indicating changes in the weather. This reflects his appreciation for a deep understanding of the environment, reminding leaders to stay aware of changing circumstances and adjust their strategies accordingly.

[Translator's Note]

In the business world, this passage could be interpreted as a call to understand the various factors that affect market conditions, such as economic indicators, technology trends, and regulatory changes. The ability to interpret these signs can help businesses anticipate and prepare for market changes.

Continuing through Chapter 9, «The Army on the March,» Sun Tzu's wisdom, translated into modern contexts, underscores the importance of understanding both competitor behavior and broader market conditions for effective strategic planning.

«When a secret piece of news is divulged by a spy before the time is ripe, he must be put to death together with the man to whom the secret was told.» - Sun Tzu

Sun Tzu addresses the consequences of a spy divulging information prematurely, stressing the importance of timing and discretion in strategic operations.

[Translator's Note]

In modern business, this can serve as a reminder about the importance of confidentiality, especially when dealing with sensitive company information or strategic plans. The premature leak of information can have significant repercussions for a business, emphasizing the need for strict controls and penalties to protect proprietary information.

«Whether the object be to crush an army, to storm a city, or to assassinate an individual, it is always necessary to begin by finding out the names of the attendants, the aides-de-camp, and door-keepers and sentries of the general in command.» - Sun Tzu

Sun Tzu underlines the value of detailed knowledge about one's enemy, right down to the personnel in lesser roles. It emphasizes thorough preparation, research, and understanding of one's adversaries.

[Translator's Note]

For businesses, this can be translated as the necessity of detailed market research, including knowledge of a competitor's structure, key employees, and strategic decision-makers. Having a comprehensive understanding of your competitors can provide critical insights and a competitive edge.

In this part of Chapter 9, «The Army on the March,» Sun Tzu's insights, when translated to contemporary business contexts, provide guidance on information confidentiality, the importance of detailed competitor research, and thorough strategic planning.

«Our spies must be commissioned to ascertain these.» - Sun Tzu

Sun Tzu underlines the importance of spies in gathering information, emphasizing the use of various methods to understand enemy strategies.

[Translator's Note]

In the corporate world, this echoes the importance of market research and competitive analysis. Businesses often use tools like market reports, customer reviews, and public data to understand competitors' strategies and anticipate market shifts.

«The enemy's spies who have come to spy on us must be sought out, tempted with bribes, led away and comfortably housed. Thus they will become double agents and available for our service.» - Sun Tzu

Sun Tzu provides a clever strategy for dealing with enemy spies. Instead of eliminating them, he suggests turning them into double agents to serve your own purposes.

[Translator's Note]

This can be translated to the business context as a strategic hiring move. A company might hire talent from competitors, not only for their skills but also for their knowledge of the competitor's operations and strategies.

Continuing through Chapter 9, «The Army on the March,» Sun Tzu's teachings, applied to modern business scenarios, reinforce the importance of comprehensive market research, competitive analysis, and strategic recruitment for gaining an edge in today's competitive business environment.

«It is through the information brought by the double agent that we are able to acquire and employ local and inward spies.» - Sun Tzu

Sun Tzu explains the value of double agents in securing more information about the enemy, illustrating the intricate and layered nature of strategic espionage in warfare.

[Translator's Note]

In the business world, this could be compared to acquiring inside information about a competitor's operations through strategic partnerships or collaborations. While ethical considerations must always be respected, understanding your competition in-depth can provide strategic insights that inform decision-making and strategy.

«It is owing to his information, again, that we can cause the doomed spy to carry false tidings to the enemy.» - Sun Tzu

Sun Tzu introduces the concept of using misinformation as a strategic tool, demonstrating the complex layers of strategy in war.

[Translator's Note]

This concept might be seen in business scenarios where companies purposely leak 'misinformation' to mislead competitors. However, this is a highly risky strategy and can lead to ethical and legal issues. It is important for businesses to always operate within the framework of the law and ethical guidelines.

As we progress through Chapter 9, «The Army on the March,» Sun Tzu's insights, when translated into modern business contexts, provide valuable lessons about strategic information gathering and the cautious use of information as a competitive tool. Ethical considerations must always be paramount.

«Lastly, it is by his information that the surviving spy can be used on appointed occasions.» - Sun Tzu

Sun Tzu highlights the usefulness of a double agent in executing specific tasks or missions. This underlines the importance of having inside information at your disposal.

[Translator's Note]

In a business scenario, this could be compared to using insights obtained from market research, customer feedback, or competitive analysis to make strategic decisions or undertake specific initiatives. Information is a powerful tool in any scenario and can provide a significant advantage when used effectively.

«The end and aim of spying in all its five varieties is knowledge of the enemy; and this knowledge can only be derived, in the first instance, from the double agent.» - Sun Tzu

Sun Tzu ends this section by reaffirming the goal of espionage: to gain knowledge of the enemy. He emphasizes the importance of the double agent as a source of this knowledge.

[Translator's Note]

This again stresses the importance of knowledge and information in the business context. Knowledge about competitors, markets, and customer preferences can provide a strategic advantage. However, it's important to ensure that this information is obtained ethically and legally.

As we wrap up this section of Chapter 9, «The Army on the March,» Sun Tzu's wisdom, when applied to the business world, underlines the importance of knowledge and information as critical strategic assets. The method of acquisition and use of this knowledge must always be guided by ethical considerations and legal compliance.

«Hence it is that which none in the whole army are more intimate relations to be maintained than with spies. None should be more liberally rewarded. In no other business should greater secrecy be preserved.» - Sun Tzu

Sun Tzu reinforces the importance of spies in warfare, emphasizing that they should be valued and rewarded for the critical information they provide. He also stresses the need for utmost secrecy in their operations.

[Translator's Not]

In a modern business context, this can be seen as a call to value employees or partners who provide essential market or competitor insights. It underscores the importance of confidentiality in strategic business matters. This could also suggest rewarding those who contribute significantly to the business's knowledge base and strategic positioning.

«Spies cannot be usefully employed without a certain intuitive sagacity; they cannot be properly managed without benevolence and straightforwardness. Without subtle ingenuity of mind, one cannot make certain of the truth of their reports.» - Sun Tzu

Sun Tzu emphasizes that effectively employing and managing spies requires wisdom, benevolence, straightforwardness, and the ability to discern truth from falsehood.

[Translator's Note]

For businesses, this underlines the need for insightful leadership and good judgment, particularly when interpreting market trends, customer feedback, or competitor activities. It also stresses the importance of integrity and fair treatment in managing relationships, whether with employees, partners, or other stakeholders.

As we continue through Chapter 9, «The Army on the March,» Sun Tzu's wisdom, when applied to the business world, emphasizes the value of information, the importance of confidentiality, and the need for insightful leadership, fair treatment, and integrity in strategic operations.

«Be subtle! be subtle! and use your spies for every kind of business.» - Sun Tzu

Sun Tzu advises leaders to be tactful and to use spies for all kinds of tasks. He highlights the diverse range of situations in which espionage can provide useful insights.

[Translator's Note]

In a business context, this can reflect the importance of being nuanced and discreet when conducting market research, competitive analysis, or customer surveys. It's also a reminder of the wide range of contexts in which these techniques can yield beneficial insights for the business.

«If a secret piece of news is divulged by a spy before the time is ripe, he must be put to death together with the man to whom the secret was told.» - Sun Tzu

This passage underscores the severe consequences of premature information leakage in a military context.

[Translator's Note]

In the corporate world, this underlines the importance of safeguarding sensitive information and maintaining the timing of strategic disclosures. It also stresses the potential severe consequences for both the source and recipient of leaked information, which could range from legal implications to loss of trust and reputation damage.

As we continue our journey through Chapter 9, «The Army on the March,» the wisdom of Sun Tzu, when applied to contemporary business, reinforces the need for discretion in business dealings, the broad applicability of information-gathering techniques, and the importance of information security and strategic timing in corporate communications.

«Whether the object be to crush an army, to storm a city, or to assassinate an individual, it is always necessary to begin by finding out the names of the attendants, the aides-de-camp, and door-keepers and sentries of the general in command.» - Sun Tzu

Sun Tzu asserts the need for comprehensive knowledge about one's target, down to the seemingly minor details. This level of detailed understanding allows for a complete understanding of the enemy and thus a more effective plan of action.

[Translator's Note]

For businesses, this could mean undertaking a comprehensive analysis of a competitor's organizational structure, key decision-makers, product lines, marketing strategies, and any other relevant information. This meticulous understanding can provide critical insights that can be utilized in forming strategies and plans.

«Our spies must be commissioned to ascertain these.» - Sun Tzu

Sun Tzu underlines the importance of having dedicated resources for gathering information, further emphasizing the critical role of information gathering in strategic planning and execution.

[Translator's Note]

In the business world, this could be seen as a recommendation to invest in market research, competitive analysis, and other forms of information gathering. This investment can yield valuable data that can inform strategic decision-making and operational planning.

As we delve further into Chapter 9, «The Army on the March,» Sun Tzu's wisdom, when translated into the world of business, underscores the importance of a thorough understanding of competitors and the strategic value of investing in information gathering.

«The enemy's spies who have come to spy on us must be sought out, tempted with bribes, led away and comfortably housed. Thus they will become double agents and available for our service.»
- Sun Tzu

Sun Tzu details a counterintelligence strategy here, using enemy spies as double agents to turn the tide in one's favor.

[Translator's Note]

In a business setting, this could be compared to talent acquisition from competing companies. Instead of just viewing these employees as potential threats, they could be seen as assets with valuable insight into the competitor's strategies, processes, and culture.

«It is through the information brought by the double agent that we are able to acquire and employ local and inward spies.» - Sun Tzu

Sun Tzu describes how the utilization of a double agent can assist in the recruitment and employment of more spies, helping to further increase the breadth and depth of intelligence gathering.

[Translator's Note]

This can be seen in a business context where a new hire from a competitor might help a company gain more industry contacts or even attract more talent from the same competitor, thereby increasing the company's competitive intelligence and strength.

As we advance in Chapter 9, «The Army on the March,» Sun Tzu's teachings, when applied to a modern business scenario, bring out the strategic importance of talent acquisition from competitors and the potential benefits of industry networking.

«It is owing to his information, again, that we can cause the doomed spy to carry false tidings to the enemy.» - Sun Tzu

Sun Tzu discusses the manipulation of information and the use of misinformation as a strategy. The double agent's information allows them to mislead the enemy by providing them with false information.

[Translator's Note]

In a business context, this strategy needs to be considered carefully due to ethical and legal considerations. Misinformation can sometimes be unintentionally spread due to misunderstandings or errors, but intentional misleading can have serious consequences, including legal repercussions.

«Lastly, it is by his information that the surviving spy can be used on appointed occasions.» - Sun Tzu

Sun Tzu indicates that the information obtained from a double agent can be used strategically at the right times. The surviving spy refers to an agent that has not been discovered or eliminated and can still be of use.

[Translator's Note]

This notion can be related to business by how information is used and when. Timely use of market research, competitive analysis, or customer insights can make a significant difference in the outcomes of marketing campaigns, product launches, and other business initiatives.

As we continue our journey through Chapter 9, «The Army on the March,» the wisdom of Sun Tzu, when applied to contemporary business, underlines the importance of strategic use of information and the potential pitfalls of misinformation..

«The end and aim of spying in all its five varieties is knowledge of the enemy; and this knowledge can only be derived, in the first instance, from the double agent.» - Sun Tzu

Sun Tzu sums up the purpose of all types of spying - to gain knowledge about the enemy. He emphasizes that the primary source of this information is often the double agent.

[Translator's Note]

In a business context, this emphasizes the importance of having a deep understanding of your competitors. This information could be sourced from multiple places, including market analysis, news reports, industry analysis, or in some cases, employees who have worked at competitor companies.

«Hence it is that which none in the whole army are more intimate relations to be maintained than with spies. None should be more liberally rewarded. In no other business should greater secrecy be preserved.» - Sun Tzu

Here, Sun Tzu highlights the value of spies in military strategy, emphasizing the need for close relationships, generous rewards, and absolute secrecy.

[Translator's Note]

This can be translated into the business realm as a reminder to value the sources of key business intelligence. This could mean maintaining good relationships with market research firms, industry analysts, or team members who provide crucial insights. It also underscores the importance of keeping strategic plans confidential.

As we reach the conclusion of Chapter 9, «The Army on the March,» we can see that Sun Tzu's insights, when applied to a modern business context, underscore the significance of competitor analysis, the value of key sources of business intelligence, and the need for secrecy in strategic plans.

Chapter 10, «Terrain.

«Sun Tzu said: We may distinguish six kinds of terrain, to wit: (1) Accessible ground; (2) entangling ground; (3) temporizing ground; (4) narrow passes; (5) precipitous heights; (6) positions at a great distance from the enemy.» - Sun Tzu

Sun Tzu lays out six types of terrain that armies may encounter, each with their unique strategic considerations.

[Translator's Note]

In a business setting, the «terrain» might be seen as the market conditions a company operates in. Just like the physical terrain in warfare, market conditions can vary greatly. For instance:

Accessible ground: This could represent a market that is easy to enter, with few barriers.

Entangling ground: This might be a market that is complex and challenging to navigate, perhaps due to convoluted regulations.

Temporizing ground: This might be a market with a lot of uncertainties where companies may want to bide their time.

Narrow passes: These could represent bottlenecks or limited opportunities in the market.

Precipitous heights: This might be a dominant market position a company has achieved.

Positions at a great distance from the enemy: This could represent untapped markets or areas where competitors are yet to establish a presence.

«Ground which can be freely traversed by both sides is called accessible. With regard to ground of this nature, be before the enemy in occupying the raised and sunny spots, and carefully guard your line of supplies. Then you will be able to fight with advantage.» - Sun Tzu

Sun Tzu explains strategies for dealing with accessible ground, emphasizing the importance of strategic positioning and safeguarding supply lines.

[Translator's Note]

This might translate into a business scenario where a new market or segment opens that is easily accessible to all players. The «raised and sunny spots» might refer to the most lucrative opportunities or niches within this market. «Guarding your line of supplies» can be seen as safeguarding your resources, processes, and operational abilities. Being early in identifying and capitalizing on such opportunities, while ensuring the robustness of your operations, will give you a competitive advantage.

«Ground which can be abandoned but is hard to re-occupy is called entangling.» - Sun Tzu

Sun Tzu describes entangling ground as a type of terrain that once left, is challenging to reclaim.

[Translator's Note]

In business terms, this might refer to a market segment or customer base that, once abandoned or neglected, could be tough to win back. This can serve as a reminder for businesses to think carefully about the potential long-term implications of their strategic moves.

As we progress in Chapter 10, «Terrain,» the wisdom of Sun Tzu, when applied to contemporary business, teaches us about the strategic considerations in different market scenarios and the importance of proactive moves and long-term thinking.

«From a position of this sort, if the enemy is unprepared, you may sally forth and defeat him. But if the enemy is prepared for your coming, and you fail to defeat him, then, return being impossible, disaster will ensue.» - Sun Tzu

Sun Tzu explains the potential outcomes on entangling ground. If the enemy is unprepared, you can gain an advantage; however, if they are prepared and you cannot defeat them, withdrawal is not an option, and failure is likely.

[Translator's Note]

In business terms, this could refer to an attempt to re-enter a market segment or regain a customer base that was previously abandoned. If the competition is unprepared, there may be an opportunity for success. However, if the competition is prepared and a company's efforts are insufficient to regain its position, it may find itself unable to retreat and facing significant losses or even a reputational disaster.

As we progress in Chapter 10, «Terrain,» the wisdom of Sun Tzu, when applied to contemporary business, teaches us about the strategic considerations in different market scenarios and the importance of proactive moves and long-term thinking..

«From a position of this sort, if the enemy is unprepared, you may sally forth and defeat him. But if the enemy is prepared for your coming, and you fail to defeat him, then, return being impossible, disaster will ensue.» - Sun Tzu

Sun Tzu explains the potential outcomes on entangling ground. If the enemy is unprepared, you can gain an advantage; however, if they are prepared and you cannot defeat them, withdrawal is not an option, and failure is likely.

[Translator's Note]

In business terms, this could refer to an attempt to re-enter a market segment or regain a customer base that was previously abandoned. If the competition is unprepared, there may be an opportunity for success. However, if the competition is prepared and a company's efforts are insufficient to regain its position, it may find itself unable to retreat and facing significant losses or even a reputational disaster.

«When the position is such that neither side will gain by making the first move, it is called temporizing ground.» - Sun Tzu

Sun Tzu identifies temporizing ground as a situation where neither side benefits from acting first, hence potentially leading to a standoff.

In a business context, this could refer to a market scenario where the first-mover advantage does not exist or where making the first move might even be detrimental, such as in certain competitive bidding scenarios or price wars. In such situations, patience and careful observation of competitors' actions could prove to be a better strategy.

As we continue our journey through Chapter 10, «Terrain,» the teachings of Sun Tzu, when applied to the modern business world, provide valuable insights on strategic decision-making in different market conditions.

«In a position of this sort, even though the enemy should offer us an attractive bait, it will be advisable not to stir forth, but rather to retreat, thus enticing the enemy in his turn; then, when part of his army has come out, we may deliver our attack with advantage.» - Sun Tzu

In this strategy, Sun Tzu suggests that in certain situations it is wiser to retreat and draw the enemy out, rather than taking the bait and potentially walking into a trap. Once the enemy is exposed or divided, a counterattack can be executed more successfully.

[Translator's Note]

From a business perspective, this could translate into not rushing to match a competitor's offer or reacting to their strategies immediately. Instead, a business might benefit more from carefully assessing the situation, perhaps even stepping back temporarily, to understand the competitor's strategy better. Once the competitor's tactics are revealed or if they overextend themselves, the business can counter with a more effective strategy of their own.

«With regard to narrow passes, if you can occupy them first, let them be strongly garrisoned and await the advent of the enemy.» - Sun Tzu

Sun Tzu advises on how to handle narrow passes in the terrain. If you can secure these strategic points first, you should fortify them and wait for the enemy to arrive.

[Translator's Note]

In a business analogy, «narrow passes» could be significant strategic opportunities that only a few competitors can exploit simultaneously, such as a lucrative contract, a partnership with a major distributor, or even hiring a highly sought-after employee. If a company can secure these opportunities first, it should consolidate its position and prepare for competitive reactions.

Continuing through Chapter 10, «Terrain,» we see how Sun Tzu's ancient wisdom can provide valuable insights into modern business strategies, teaching us the importance of patience, analysis, and strategic consolidation in various competitive situations.

«Should the army forestall you in occupying a pass, do not go after him if the pass is fully garrisoned, but only if it is weakly garrisoned.» - Sun Tzu

Sun Tzu suggests that if an enemy beats you to a strategic position and strongly fortifies it, it's not wise to attack. Only if their defenses are weak should you consider engaging.

[Translator's Note]

In a business scenario, this could refer to a situation where a competitor has already secured a strategic advantage, such as an exclusive contract or key distribution channel. If their position is strong, it might not be effective to challenge them directly. Instead, looking for alternative opportunities or waiting until their position weakens might be more strategic.

«With regard to precipitous heights, if you are beforehand with your adversary, you should occupy the raised and sunny spots, and there wait for him to come up.» - Sun Tzu

On precipitous heights, Sun Tzu advises occupying the high and sunny spots before the enemy arrives and waiting for them there.

[Translator's Note]

In business, «precipitous heights» can be likened to high-value opportunities or market positions. If a company gets there first, it should secure its position and prepare for competitors who may try to challenge it. The «raised and sunny spots» could represent aspects such as market share, brand recognition, or superior product features.

As we continue with Chapter 10, «Terrain,» Sun Tzu's strategies, when applied to business, remind us of the importance of strategic positioning, recognizing the strength of competitors, and proactively securing high-value opportunities..

«If the enemy has occupied them before you, do not follow him, but retreat and try to entice him away.» - Sun Tzu

Sun Tzu advises against trying to take over precipitous heights that the enemy has already secured. Instead, he suggests retreating and attempting to lure the enemy away from their advantageous position.

[Translator's Note]

In a business context, this might apply when a competitor has already secured a strong position in a high-value market segment or established a dominant brand. Directly challenging the competitor in this case may not be effective. Instead, a more strategic approach could be to focus on other areas, possibly drawing the competitor's resources away from their stronghold, and then exploiting any opportunities this creates.

«If you are situated at a great distance from the enemy, and the strength of the two armies is equal, it is not easy to provoke a battle, and fighting will be to your disadvantage.» - Sun Tzu

Sun Tzu notes the difficulties in provoking a battle when situated far from the enemy, especially when both armies have similar strengths. In such a case, engaging in combat could put you at a disadvantage.

[Translator's Note]

In terms of business, this could be interpreted as trying to compete in a market where your business has no presence or influence, especially when the competition has equivalent resources and capabilities. Attempting to provoke a market battle in such a scenario can lead to wasted resources and potentially harm your company.

As we continue with Chapter 10, «Terrain,» we can further appreciate how Sun Tzu's ancient military wisdom can be translated into modern business strategies. His lessons remind us of the value of strategic maneuvering, understanding competitive dynamics, and making decisions based on one's relative position and capabilities.

«These six are the principles connected with Earth. The general who has attained a responsible post must be careful to study them.» - Sun Tzu

Sun Tzu concludes his teachings on different types of terrains, emphasizing the importance of understanding these principles for anyone in a position of leadership.

[Translator's Note]

In business, these «principles connected with Earth» can translate to understanding the different market terrains and the strategic implications they hold. Any business leader should study these principles carefully to navigate effectively through competitive scenarios and make informed decisions.

«Now an army is exposed to six several calamities, not arising from natural causes, but from faults for which the general is responsible.» - Sun Tzu

Sun Tzu begins a new topic, focusing on the calamities that can befall an army due to errors made by its general.

[Translator's Note]

In the business context, these «six calamities» could represent the significant mistakes a business leader might make, leading to problems for the organization. It emphasizes the significant role and responsibility of leadership in determining an organization's success or failure.

As we close Chapter 10, «Terrain,» and start a new topic, we learn from Sun Tzu about the importance of understanding one's environment and the leader's role in avoiding mistakes that can harm the organization. These lessons remain as relevant today as they were in ancient times, providing valuable insights for modern business leadership.

«These are: (1) Flight; (2) insubordination; (3) collapse; (4) ruin; (5) disorganization; (6) rout.» - Sun Tzu

Sun Tzu lists the six calamities that an army can suffer due to errors from its general.

[Translator's Note]

In a business scenario, these calamities could be interpreted as follows:

Flight: a rapid decline in business, leading to retreat or withdrawal from the market.

Insubordination: lack of alignment within the team, leading to disobedience and lack of coordination.

Collapse: a sudden and total failure in the business, such as bankruptcy.

Ruin: severe damage to the business that compromises its structure and functioning.

Disorganization: a lack of order or systematic arrangement within the business, leading to inefficiency and confusion.

Rout: a complete defeat, where the business is overwhelmed by its competitors.

«Other conditions being equal, if one force is hurled against another ten times its size, the result will be the flight of the former.»
- Sun Tzu

Sun Tzu acknowledges the numerical superiority in a battle. If a smaller force is pitted against a force ten times its size, it will likely flee.

[Translator's Note]

From a business standpoint, this could be seen as a smaller company or startup attempting to compete directly with a significantly larger or established enterprise. If they do not have a unique differentiator or strategy, the smaller company may quickly find itself overwhelmed and forced to retreat.

As we delve into these new topics in Sun Tzu's teachings, we can further understand the pitfalls in leadership and strategy that can lead to failure in both military and business contexts. Understanding these risks can help us prevent them and steer our organizations towards success.

«When the common soldiers are too strong and their officers too weak, the result is insubordination.» - Sun Tzu

Sun Tzu points out that if the soldiers are stronger than their officers, insubordination may arise, disrupting order and command in the army.

[Translator's Note]

In the corporate world, this might be likened to a situation where the employees do not respect or follow their managers due to perceived incompetence or weakness. This lack of leadership can lead to disobedience, lack of coordination, and reduced productivity.

«When the officers are too strong and the common soldiers too weak, the result is collapse.» - Sun Tzu

Conversely, Sun Tzu warns that an overly strong officer cadre with weak soldiers can lead to collapse. If the army's core is weak, it cannot support strong leaders, and the entire structure may crumble.

[Translator's Note]

In a business context, this could refer to a company with strong leaders but weak employees or infrastructure. A business cannot thrive if its foundational elements are weak, no matter how strong or competent its leaders are. It highlights the importance of strengthening all levels within an organization, from leadership to frontline employees.

Continuing with Sun Tzu's teachings on leadership and organization, we gain valuable insights into the balance of power and strength in any organization, military or business. These insights stress the importance of both strong leadership and a strong workforce, providing lessons for today's business leaders in managing their teams effectively.

«When the higher officers are angry and insubordinate, and on meeting the enemy give battle on their own account from a feeling of resentment, before the commander-in-chief can tell whether or not he is in a position to fight, the result is ruin.» - Sun Tzu

Sun Tzu highlights a critical calamity caused by the insubordination and impulsiveness of higher officers. If they choose to engage the enemy out of anger, without the knowledge or consent of the commander-in-chief, the result can be catastrophic.

[Translator's Note]

In a business context, this scenario could translate to senior managers making hasty decisions out of personal sentiments or ego, without aligning with the company's overall strategic plan. This could result in severe consequences for the business, including loss of resources, damaged relationships, or missed opportunities. It underlines the importance of unity in command and alignment in strategy at all levels of management.

«When the general is weak and without authority; when his orders are not clear and distinct; when there are no fixed duties assigned to officers and men, and the ranks are formed in a slovenly haphazard manner, the result is utter disorganization.» - Sun Tzu

Sun Tzu underlines the role of the general's authority and clarity in his commands. A weak general with unclear orders and poorly defined roles for his subordinates leads to chaos and disorganization.

[Translator's Note]

This mirrors situations in businesses where leadership lacks decisiveness, clarity in communication, and fails to define clear roles and responsibilities for the team members. This lack of organizational structure can result in inefficiencies, confusion, and poor performance. Effective leadership and clear communication are thus key to a well-functioning organization.

As we delve deeper into Sun Tzu's teachings, it becomes evident how his military strategies translate to business lessons, emphasizing effective leadership, strategic alignment, clear communication, and well-defined roles for a successful organization.

«When a general, unable to estimate the enemy's strength, allows an inferior force to engage a larger one, or hurls a weak detachment against a powerful one, and neglects to place picked soldiers in the front rank, the result must be rout.» - Sun Tzu

Sun Tzu warns of the consequences of a general's failure to correctly estimate the enemy's strength, leading to situations where weaker forces confront stronger ones, causing total defeat or rout.

[Translator's Note]

From a business standpoint, this can be likened to a situation where a leader fails to properly assess the competition's strength and thus engages in competition recklessly. This lack of strategic assessment can result in the business being overwhelmed by competitors. It underscores the importance of competitive analysis and strategic planning in business operations.

«These are six ways of courting defeat, which must be carefully noted by the general who has attained a responsible post.» - Sun Tzu

Sun Tzu concludes his teachings on the six calamities, reemphasizing their importance for a leader to understand and avoid.

[Translator's Note]

In business, these «six ways of courting defeat» serve as a reminder for leaders to avoid common pitfalls that could lead to business failure. The lessons emphasize the importance of understanding the competitive landscape, maintaining organizational discipline and balance, clear communication, and the effective allocation of resources.

With the close of Sun Tzu's teachings on the six calamities, we gain critical insights into strategic errors that leaders must avoid. These ancient military lessons offer modern business leaders valuable guidance on effective leadership and strategic management.

«The natural formation of the country is the soldier's best ally; but a power of estimating the adversary, of controlling the forces of victory, and of shrewdly calculating difficulties, dangers and distances, constitutes the test of a great general.» - Sun Tzu

Sun Tzu highlights the importance of understanding one's environment and the ability to accurately assess the adversary. These qualities, along with the ability to control victory's forces and calculate risks and distances, make a great general.

[Translator's Note]

In the business world, understanding the market environment and assessing competitors effectively are paramount for success. Moreover, a leader's ability to control the variables leading to victory—resources, strategy, team performance—and to calculate risks and opportunities are essential traits for successful business management.

«He who knows these things, and in fighting puts his knowledge into practice, will win his battles. He who knows them not, nor practices them, will surely be defeated.» - Sun Tzu

Sun Tzu emphasizes the value of knowledge and the application of that knowledge in winning battles. Those who fail to learn and apply these principles will be defeated.

[Translator's Note]

From a business perspective, the application of strategic knowledge in real-life scenarios is critical to success. Companies that invest in learning about their industry, competitors, and market trends and apply this knowledge to their strategies will be more successful than those who do not.

Sun Tzu's wisdom continues to illuminate the path to victory, both on the battlefield and in the boardroom. The value of understanding one's environment, assessing the adversary effectively, and applying this knowledge in practice remains timeless and universal.

«If fighting is sure to result in victory, then you must fight, even though the ruler forbid it; if fighting will not result in victory, then you must not fight even at the ruler's bidding.» - Sun Tzu

Sun Tzu presents a bold view on defiance for the sake of victory. He suggests that a general should engage in battle if victory is certain, even against the ruler's orders. Conversely, if defeat is certain, a general should avoid battle, even if the ruler demands it.

[Translator's Note]

In the business context, this underlines the importance of strategic autonomy and the courage to take decisions that contradict higher authority when they are in the best interest of the organization. Similarly, it's important to resist engaging in unprofitable ventures, despite pressure from above. This principle emphasizes the value of informed decision-making and strategic leadership.

«The general who advances without coveting fame and retreats without fearing disgrace, whose only thought is to protect his country and do good service for his sovereign, is the jewel of the kingdom.» - Sun Tzu

Sun Tzu extols the virtues of a selfless general who is driven not by personal ambition or fear of disgrace, but by the sole purpose of serving his country and sovereign. This kind of leader, he declares, is truly precious.

[Translator's Note]

In modern organizations, leaders who act with the company's best interests in mind, rather than personal ambition, and who aren't deterred by the fear of failure, are indeed valuable. These selfless leaders put the organization's needs first and can significantly contribute to its success.

Through these reflections, Sun Tzu introduces the value of strategic defiance, the importance of acting in the best interest of the organization, and the priceless worth of selfless leadership. These lessons resonate profoundly in today's business world, reminding us of the timeless value of strategic wisdom and principled leadership.

«Regard your soldiers as your children, and they will follow you into the deepest valleys; look upon them as your own beloved sons, and they will stand by you even unto death.» - Sun Tzu

Sun Tzu emphasizes the power of compassion and empathy in leadership. By treating soldiers with the care and affection of a parent, a leader can inspire unwavering loyalty and devotion, enabling them to follow even in the face of grave danger.

[Translator's Note]

In business, this could be applied to the relationship between a leader and their team. By treating team members with empathy, showing care for their well-being and professional growth, a leader can cultivate loyalty and dedication. This can result in a high-performing team that is committed even in challenging circumstances.

«If, however, you are indulgent, but unable to make your authority felt; kind-hearted, but unable to enforce your commands; and incapable, moreover, of quelling disorder: then your soldiers must be likened to spoilt children; they are useless for any practical purpose.» - Sun Tzu

While advocating for compassion in leadership, Sun Tzu also warns of the dangers of excessive leniency without discipline. If a leader cannot maintain authority and order, their troops become akin to spoiled children, useless in practical situations.

[Translator's Note]

This advice holds true in modern business environments as well. While it is important for leaders to be empathetic and kind, it's equally crucial to maintain authority, enforce standards, and manage team dynamics effectively. A balance of kindness and discipline often leads to a productive and harmonious work environment.

These teachings from Sun Tzu demonstrate the delicate balance in leadership between showing empathy and maintaining authority, underlining the importance of cultivating loyalty and discipline within a team. These principles remain as relevant today in modern business leadership as they were on the ancient battlefields.

«If we know that our own men are in a condition to attack, but are unaware that the enemy is not open to attack, we have gone only halfway towards victory.» - Sun Tzu

Sun Tzu articulates the need for complete understanding in battle, emphasizing that knowing one's own strength is insufficient. A comprehensive assessment of the enemy's weaknesses is equally crucial to securing victory.

[Translator's Note]

This insight can be applied to business strategy. It's not enough to understand your organization's strengths and readiness to undertake a venture; it's equally important to understand the market conditions, the competition's weaknesses, and the receptivity of consumers. Incomplete knowledge could lead to unsuccessful ventures, while comprehensive information can pave the way for victory in business competition.

«If we know that the enemy is open to attack, but are unaware that our own men are not in a condition to attack, we have gone only halfway towards victory.» - Sun Tzu

Continuing his thought, Sun Tzu warns that knowing the enemy's vulnerability but ignoring one's own readiness for battle also only leads halfway towards victory.

[Translator's Note]

This again emphasizes the need for a full perspective in business. A company might see an opportunity to disrupt a market or launch a new product, but if it doesn't consider its own readiness—in terms of resources, personnel, infrastructure, or other necessary conditions—it could lead to failure. Thus, self-awareness and market awareness are both essential for strategic planning.

Sun Tzu's teachings on the complete understanding of one's own and the enemy's conditions underpin the essence of successful strategy. These principles can guide modern business strategies, reminding leaders of the value of comprehensive knowledge and balanced perspective in decision-making.

«If we know that the enemy is open to attack, and also know that our men are in a condition to attack, but are unaware that the nature of the ground makes fighting impracticable, we have still gone only halfway towards victory.» - Sun Tzu

Sun Tzu reiterates that knowing your capabilities and your enemy's vulnerabilities is insufficient if you don't consider the environment or 'the ground.' The nature of the battleground could make a seemingly advantageous fight untenable.

[Translator's Note]

In the realm of business, 'the ground' could be considered as market conditions or external factors. Understanding your organization's strengths and your competitor's weaknesses is not enough. You must also be cognizant of market trends, regulatory changes, or other external factors that could impact the success of your strategy.

«Hence the experienced soldier, once in motion, is never bewildered; once he has broken camp, he is never at a loss.» - Sun Tzu

Sun Tzu lauds the experienced soldier who, because of his understanding and preparation, is never perplexed or lost once he initiates action.

[Translator's Note]

In business, experience and preparation are invaluable. Leaders who are well-prepared and have learned from past experiences are less likely to be caught off guard or unsure once they set their strategies in motion. This speaks to the importance of experience, planning, and adaptability in business leadership.

Through these insights, Sun Tzu teaches the importance of considering all factors in a strategy - our capabilities, the enemy's weaknesses, and the environment. He also emphasizes the value of experience and preparation in executing strategy. These principles continue to guide strategic decision-making in business environments today.

«Hence the saying: If you know the enemy and know yourself, you need not fear the result of a hundred battles. If you know yourself but not the enemy, for every victory gained you will also suffer a defeat. If you know neither the enemy nor yourself, you will succumb in every battle.» - Sun Tzu

Sun Tzu concisely sums up the wisdom of strategic knowledge. By knowing both oneself and the enemy, a leader can confidently engage in conflict. However, a lack of knowledge about either oneself or the enemy can lead to unstable victories or even defeat.

[Translator's Note]

This maxim applies as much to business as it did to ancient warfare. Companies must understand their strengths and weaknesses, as well as those of their competitors, to navigate market competition successfully. Ignorance of either leads to instability, and ignorance of both can lead to failure. It underscores the importance of continuous learning, market research, and self-assessment in business.

«Move not unless you see an advantage; use not your troops unless there is something to be gained; fight not unless the position is critical.» - Sun Tzu

Sun Tzu offers tactical advice, recommending caution and strategic calculation. Leaders should not move without seeing an advantage, not deploy their troops without something to gain, and not engage in battle unless absolutely necessary.

[Translator's Note]

This advice can guide business decisions as well. Companies should not undertake initiatives without clear advantages or benefits, should not allocate resources without the prospect of gain, and should not engage in market battles unless their position is threatened or the opportunity is critical. It emphasizes prudence, strategic allocation of resources, and calculated risks in business.

Through these nuggets of wisdom, Sun Tzu offers invaluable advice on strategic knowledge and careful planning, lessons that hold relevance not just on the battlefield but also in the boardroom. His teachings continue to guide leaders in making informed and strategic decisions in business.

«No ruler should put troops into the field merely to gratify his own spleen; no general should fight a battle simply out of pique.» - Sun Tzu

Sun Tzu cautions leaders against letting personal emotions dictate strategic decisions. He warns against deploying troops or engaging in battles out of spite or anger.

[Translator's Note]

This wisdom translates well to modern business environments. Leaders should not make strategic decisions based on personal emotions or ego. Such decisions could lead to misallocation of resources or unnecessary conflicts, damaging the organization in the long run. Decisions should be made objectively, based on what is best for the organization and its stakeholders.

«If it is to your advantage, make a forward move; if not, stay where you are.» - Sun Tzu

Sun Tzu advises leaders to make proactive moves only when they provide a clear advantage. If no such advantage is present, maintaining the current position is the recommended course.

[Translator's Note]

In business, this advice encourages leaders to pursue growth and take risks only when they offer clear benefits. If the risks outweigh the potential gains or if the current state of affairs is beneficial, it can be wise to maintain the status quo. This underscores the importance of strategic patience and careful evaluation in business decision-making.

Sun Tzu's teachings highlight the importance of emotional intelligence, strategic patience, and objective decision-making for effective leadership. These principles, dating back thousands of years, are timeless in their wisdom and are as applicable in modern business leadership as they were on ancient battlefields.

«Anger may in time change to gladness; vexation may be succeeded by content.» - Sun Tzu

Sun Tzu acknowledges the changing nature of emotions, hinting that temporary feelings of anger or vexation should not drive long-term decisions, as these feelings can eventually turn into happiness or contentment.

[Translator's Note]

In the context of business, this insight serves as a reminder that transient negative emotions or setbacks should not dictate long-term strategy or decision-making. It underscores the importance of emotional resilience and a long-term perspective in business leadership.

«But a kingdom that has once been destroyed can never come again into being; nor can the dead ever be brought back to life.» - Sun Tzu

Sun Tzu emphasizes the permanence of certain consequences, noting that destroyed kingdoms cannot be resurrected, and the dead cannot return to life.

[Translator's Note]

From a business perspective, this statement serves as a stark reminder of the importance of protecting the integrity and survival of an organization. Severe strategic missteps or ethical failures can lead to irreversible damage. It underscores the importance of ethical conduct, sustainable practices, and risk management in business operations.

«Hence the enlightened ruler is heedful, and the good general full of caution. This is the way to keep a country at peace and an army intact.» - Sun Tzu

In conclusion, Sun Tzu advises leaders to be mindful and cautious, suggesting that these qualities help maintain peace and keep the army unharmed.

[Translator's Note]

In the business realm, this advice stresses the value of foresight, caution, and mindfulness in leadership. These traits help to maintain organizational stability and ensure its long-term survival and success.

Sun Tzu's teachings, although framed in the context of warfare, carry profound wisdom for modern business leadership. They emphasize emotional intelligence, a long-term perspective, ethical conduct, and cautious decision-making - traits that are crucial for the success and survival of organizations in today's competitive business landscape.

«In war, then, let your great object be victory, not lengthy campaigns.» - Sun Tzu

Sun Tzu asserts the primacy of victory and discourages protracted warfare. His emphasis is on swift and decisive action that leads to victory, not long-drawn conflicts.

[Translator's Note]

In business terms, this insight translates into the importance of setting clear objectives and striving for efficient and effective solutions rather than drawn-out processes. It speaks to the value of decisiveness, efficiency, and focus on outcomes in business strategy and operations.

«Thus it may be known that the leader of armies is the arbiter of the people's fate, the man on whom it depends whether the nation shall be in peace or in peril.» - Sun Tzu

Sun Tzu underlines the vital role and immense responsibility of the military leader, noting that the fate of the people and the state of the nation rest in their hands.

[Translator's Note]

In the corporate world, this principle highlights the significant role and responsibility of business leaders. The decisions they make can shape the future of the organization, influence the wellbeing of its employees, and impact its standing in the marketplace. It underscores the weight of leadership decisions and the importance of sound judgment in business leadership.

Sun Tzu's timeless wisdom continues to enlighten modern-day leaders. His teachings about victory, efficiency, and the gravity of leadership responsibility remain relevant and valuable in the ever-evolving world of business. His insights provide a unique perspective on leadership and strategy, transcending the bounds of time and context.

«In the midst of chaos, there is also opportunity.» - Sun Tzu

Sun Tzu acknowledges that even in times of disorder and confusion, opportunities can arise. He encourages leaders to stay alert and be ready to seize these opportunities when they present themselves.

[Translator's Note]

This insight is particularly relevant for businesses operating in volatile and uncertain markets. It reminds leaders to stay agile, adapt to changing circumstances, and seek opportunities even in challenging situations. This concept is fundamental to business innovation and resilience.

«Treat your men as you would your own beloved sons. And they will follow you into the deepest valley.» - Sun Tzu

Sun Tzu underscores the importance of compassionate leadership. He suggests that leaders who treat their troops with kindness and respect will earn unwavering loyalty and commitment.

[Translator's Note]

This principle remains incredibly relevant in the world of business. Leaders who treat their employees with respect, empathy, and care are more likely to foster a committed and motivated workforce. This concept forms the bedrock of positive corporate culture and employee engagement.

Sun Tzu's teachings, though articulated in the context of warfare, carry profound insights for contemporary business leadership. His observations about opportunity in chaos and compassionate leadership are principles that guide successful and sustainable business practices. They serve as reminders that strategy, humanity, and adaptability are vital to good leadership and business success.

«He will win who knows when to fight and when not to fight.»
- Sun Tzu

Sun Tzu emphasizes discernment in choosing battles. Winning, according to him, is not about engaging in every battle, but knowing when to fight and when to abstain.

[Translator's Note]

This insight is crucial in the business world, where resources are limited, and strategy is paramount. Choosing the right projects, the right markets, and the right battles is a key determinant of success. It underscores the importance of strategic focus and discretion in business leadership.

«Opportunities multiply as they are seized.» - Sun Tzu

Sun Tzu points out a virtuous cycle where seizing opportunities leads to the creation of more opportunities.

[Translator's Note]

In the business context, this observation is a testament to the power of initiative and momentum. By seizing opportunities, businesses can generate momentum that opens up further opportunities for growth and expansion. This principle reinforces the importance of proactive and opportunistic business strategy.

Through his teachings, Sun Tzu offers valuable lessons in strategic discernment and initiative. His words serve as reminders that effective leadership requires a discerning mind and a courageous spirit - attributes that stand the test of time and are as relevant in the modern business world as they were in ancient warfare.

«The supreme art of war is to subdue the enemy without fighting.» - Sun Tzu

Sun Tzu states that the highest form of warfare is not one where battles are fought and blood is shed, but one where the enemy is subdued without a fight.

[Translator's Note]

In the corporate world, this wisdom can be interpreted as achieving business objectives with minimal conflict and waste of resources. This could mean negotiating a deal with a competitor, innovating to create a unique market space, or influencing consumer behavior. It emphasizes the value of diplomacy, innovation, and strategic influence in business operations.

«He who knows when he can fight and when he cannot, will be victorious.» - Sun Tzu

Again, Sun Tzu stresses the importance of discernment in warfare. The key to victory, according to him, lies in recognizing when to engage in battle and when to refrain.

[Translator's Note]

In the business context, this principle underscores the importance of strategic assessment and discretion. It encourages business leaders to evaluate their capabilities and resources, understand the business environment, and make strategic decisions accordingly. It speaks to the essence of strategic agility and prudence in business leadership.

Sun Tzu's age-old wisdom offers deep insights into leadership and strategy that remain pertinent today. The lessons of discernment, strategic influence, and the importance of understanding one's capabilities resonate strongly with contemporary business leaders navigating complex and dynamic business landscapes. These insights continue to inform and inspire effective and strategic leadership.

«Victorious warriors win first and then go to war, while defeated warriors go to war first and then seek to win.» - Sun Tzu

Sun Tzu's words emphasize the importance of careful planning and preparation before going into battle. Winning, according to him, happens before the war even begins.

[Translator's Note]

In business terms, this principle underlines the value of proactive planning and strategy. Businesses that thoroughly plan, strategize, and prepare before venturing into new markets, launching new products, or taking on competitors are more likely to succeed. It underscores the importance of strategic foresight in business operations.

«To know your enemy, you must become your enemy.» - Sun Tzu

Sun Tzu stresses the importance of understanding the opponent. To truly know and comprehend them, one must think and strategize from their perspective.

[Translator's Note]

This concept is particularly relevant in today's competitive business environment. It encourages business leaders to gain a deep understanding of their competitors - their strategies, strengths, weaknesses, and perspectives. This knowledge is crucial for formulating effective competitive strategies. It emphasizes the importance of competitor analysis and strategic empathy in business.

Sun Tzu's teachings shed light on essential aspects of strategic thinking and preparation. His emphasis on planning and understanding the competition offers valuable insights for business leaders, reminding them that the road to success involves careful strategizing and empathetic understanding of others in the field. His timeless wisdom continues to guide leaders across different domains, transcending the battlefield to find relevance in boardrooms and beyond.

«If you know the enemy and know yourself, you need not fear the result of a hundred battles.» - Sun Tzu

Sun Tzu asserts that deep knowledge and understanding of oneself and the enemy will lead to victory, regardless of how many battles are fought.

[Translator's Note]

In the business context, knowing oneself equates to understanding the company's strengths, weaknesses, capabilities, and limits. Knowing the enemy translates to a thorough understanding of competitors, market dynamics, customer preferences, and external challenges. The combination of these two forms of knowledge can lead to strategic prowess and resilience in the face of competition and market volatility.

«The general who wins the battle makes many calculations in his temple before the battle is fought. The general who loses makes but few calculations beforehand.» - Sun Tzu

Sun Tzu emphasizes the importance of thorough planning and preparation before going into battle. Victory, according to him, is a result of careful calculations and considerations made well in advance.

[Translator's Note]

In business terms, this principle reinforces the importance of strategic planning, market analysis, and risk assessment. Businesses that make informed decisions based on rigorous analysis and foresight are more likely to succeed. It underscores the value of meticulous planning and strategy in business operations.

Sun Tzu's wisdom transcends time and context, offering invaluable insights into strategic thinking and decision-making. His emphasis on self-awareness, competitor understanding, and detailed planning provide guiding principles for modern businesses navigating a complex and competitive landscape. Sun Tzu's words serve as a timeless manual for strategic leadership in any domain.

«Even the finest sword plunged into salt water will eventually rust.» - Sun Tzu

Sun Tzu here underlines that even the best tools or skills, when placed in a harmful or unfavorable environment, will deteriorate over time.

[Translator's Note]

This statement is a potent reminder for businesses about the significance of their environment or market conditions. Even with excellent products or top-notch skills, if the business environment is not conducive, it can lead to decline. It underscores the importance of continuous market research and analysis, along with necessary adaptations and transformations.

«Strategy without tactics is the slowest route to victory. Tactics without strategy is the noise before defeat.» - Sun Tzu

Sun Tzu makes a distinction between strategy and tactics, emphasizing the importance of both. He suggests that while strategy defines the 'what' and 'why', tactics define the 'how'. Both are crucial and need to work in harmony for achieving victory.

[Translator's Note]

In the corporate world, this principle reinforces the idea that both long-term strategic planning and short-term tactical actions are essential for success. A company needs a clear vision (strategy) and an actionable plan (tactics) to achieve its goals. It stresses the importance of balancing and aligning strategic objectives with tactical execution in business operations.

Through his timeless wisdom, Sun Tzu offers profound insights into the interplay of strategy and tactics, and the impact of the environment on performance. These lessons continue to resonate with modern businesses, reminding leaders of the importance of understanding their environment, crafting clear strategies, and devising actionable tactics. His teachings serve as a guiding beacon for contemporary leadership and strategy.

«In the midst of chaos, there is also opportunity.» - Sun Tzu

Here, Sun Tzu asserts that even in chaotic situations, there is the potential for opportunity. It emphasizes the idea that crisis and opportunities often go hand-in-hand.

[Translator's Note]

In a business context, this highlights the importance of agility and resilience in the face of challenges or market disruptions. It suggests that businesses should strive to identify and seize opportunities even in turbulent times. It can be seen as a call to adopt a proactive and opportunistic approach towards problem-solving and crisis management.

Sun Tzu's teachings on the complete understanding of one's own and the enemy's conditions underpin the essence of successful strategy. These principles can guide modern business strategies, reminding leaders of the value of comprehensive knowledge and balanced perspective in decision-making.

«The wise warrior avoids the battle.» - Sun Tzu

Sun Tzu emphasizes the idea that the wisest warriors are those who can attain their objectives without physically fighting.

[Translator's Note]

From a business perspective, this can be interpreted as the importance of achieving business objectives with minimal conflict or resources. This could mean striking a favorable deal with a competitor, outmaneuvering competition through innovation, or influencing consumer behavior. It underscores the significance of diplomacy and strategic maneuvering in business operations.

Sun Tzu's words serve as a constant reminder that strategy, wisdom, and adaptation are the cornerstones of success, be it on the battlefield or in the boardroom. The ability to spot opportunities amidst chaos and the wisdom to achieve objectives without unnecessary confrontation offer valuable lessons for today's dynamic and often unpredictable business environment. His teachings continue to resonate and provide a guiding light for strategic thinking and decision-making.

«He will win who knows when to fight and when not to fight.»
- Sun Tzu

Sun Tzu emphasizes the importance of timing in warfare. Understanding when to engage and when to refrain from engagement can be the key to victory.

[Translator's Note]

In the realm of business, this principle signifies the importance of strategic timing. Deciding when to launch a product, when to enter a new market, or when to pivot in strategy can often make a significant difference in the outcomes. It underlines the importance of having a pulse on market dynamics, customer behavior, and external macro trends.

«Pretend inferiority and encourage his arrogance.» - Sun Tzu

Here, Sun Tzu highlights a deceptive strategy used to make the enemy overconfident, thus exposing their weaknesses or leading them into a trap.

[Translator's Note]

From a business perspective, this could be seen as a call to understand and leverage competitor overconfidence. By appearing less threatening, businesses may encourage competitors to make strategic blunders or overextend themselves. It reiterates the value of understanding and subtly manipulating competitive dynamics.

Sun Tzu's teachings not only outline successful strategies for warfare but also have profound implications in business leadership and strategy. His principles surrounding the timing of actions and deceptive strategies to take advantage of competitor's overconfidence are as relevant today as they were millennia ago. His profound wisdom continues to enlighten leaders, influencing strategic decisions and competitive tactics in today's dynamic business world.

«Supreme excellence consists in breaking the enemy's resistance without fighting.» - Sun Tzu

Sun Tzu emphasizes that the ultimate form of skill is not in defeating the enemy through combat, but in breaking their resistance without the need for battle.

[Translator's Note]

In business, this insight could be interpreted as the ability to outmaneuver competition without engaging in destructive price wars or direct confrontation. It might mean winning over a competitor's customer base through superior customer service, creating a superior product, or innovating in a way that makes the competitor's offerings obsolete.

«Opportunities multiply as they are seized.» - Sun Tzu

Sun Tzu points out that taking advantage of opportunities leads to the creation of more opportunities. It's a potent reminder of the snowball effect that can come from seizing the initiative.

[Translator's Note]

This is particularly relevant to businesses in fast-paced industries, where taking advantage of one opportunity often leads to others. For instance, being the first to market with a new product could lead to brand recognition, which then opens up opportunities for partnerships, expansions, and more.

The wisdom of Sun Tzu extends far beyond the battlefield, offering valuable insights for businesses navigating today's competitive landscape. The essence of his teachings—breaking the competition's resistance without direct confrontation and seizing opportunities as they present themselves—continues to offer strategic guidance to contemporary businesses. His insights remain invaluable for leaders striving for excellence in the corporate world.

«The art of war is of vital importance to the state. It is a matter of life and death, a road either to safety or to ruin.» - Sun Tzu

Sun Tzu emphasizes the crucial significance of understanding and mastering the art of war, equating it to matters of life and death, safety or ruin.

[Translator's Note]

Translating this principle to business, it underscores the vital importance of strategic planning and execution. A well-considered and executed strategy can lead to business growth and stability, whereas poor planning can lead to ruin. Businesses, like states, need to view their strategic planning with utmost seriousness and diligence.

«Victorious warriors win first and then go to war, while defeated warriors go to war first and then seek to win.» - Sun Tzu

Here, Sun Tzu highlights the importance of planning and preparation. Victorious warriors win in their planning stage and then implement their plans in the battlefield.

[Translator's Note]

In a business context, this principle highlights the importance of thorough planning and preparation before implementation. Successful companies strategize, anticipate possible challenges, prepare for different scenarios, and then launch their products or services. It emphasizes that victory is achieved first in planning and preparation.

The wisdom of Sun Tzu, as depicted in these teachings, remains crucial for contemporary businesses. Understanding the importance of strategic planning and preparation, and considering these tasks with the seriousness they deserve, can make the difference between success and failure. Sun Tzu's timeless strategies provide invaluable insights for modern business leaders navigating the complex corporate battlegrounds.

«If you know the enemy and know yourself, you need not fear the result of a hundred battles.» - Sun Tzu

This is one of Sun Tzu's most famous quotes. It emphasizes the importance of understanding oneself and one's enemies (or competitors) to ensure victory in any conflict.

[Translator's Note]

In the world of business, this quote reinforces the need for thorough market research and self-awareness. Understanding your own company's strengths and weaknesses, as well as those of your competitors, is vital for strategic planning. This insight can guide companies in creating competitive products, effective marketing strategies, and sound business decisions.

«In the midst of chaos, there is also opportunity.» - Sun Tzu

Sun Tzu asserts that even in chaotic situations, there is the potential for opportunity. It emphasizes the idea that crisis and opportunities often go hand-in-hand.

[Translator's Note]

In a business context, this highlights the importance of agility and resilience in the face of challenges or market disruptions. It suggests that businesses should strive to identify and seize opportunities even in turbulent times. It can be seen as a call to adopt a proactive and opportunistic approach towards problem-solving and crisis management.

The teachings of Sun Tzu, though rooted in the context of ancient warfare, offer timeless wisdom that remains relevant in today's business world. The importance of understanding oneself and one's competition, as well as the ability to find opportunities amidst chaos, are principles that modern-day leaders can apply to navigate their businesses towards success. His wisdom continues to provide a guiding light for strategic thinking and decision-making.

«He will win who, prepared himself, waits to take the enemy unprepared.» - Sun Tzu

Sun Tzu is underscoring the value of preparation and the element of surprise in achieving victory. The one who is ready and waits for the perfect moment to strike an unprepared enemy will prevail.

[Translator's Note]

In business, this could be viewed as the importance of strategic foresight and preparation. It can also refer to the element of surprise in a market through innovation, unveiling a new product or service that competitors are unprepared for. Timing and preparation often differentiate successful businesses from unsuccessful ones.

«Even the finest sword plunged into salt water will eventually rust.» - Sun Tzu

Sun Tzu here conveys that even the most effective tools or strategies will degrade if exposed to unfavorable conditions for extended periods.

[Translator's Note]

From a business perspective, this lesson reminds us of the importance of adaptability and innovation. Even the most successful products, services, or business models may become outdated or ineffective in changing market conditions. Continuous innovation and adaptation are key to maintaining a competitive edge in the ever-evolving business landscape.

These teachings from Sun Tzu provide valuable insights that are as applicable to the business leaders of today as they were to the generals of ancient times. From understanding the power of preparation and surprise to recognizing the need for continual innovation in changing environments, his wisdom continues to influence strategic decision-making in today's complex and dynamic world.

«Strategy without tactics is the slowest route to victory. Tactics without strategy is the noise before defeat.» - Sun Tzu

Sun Tzu delineates the complementary relationship between strategy and tactics, pointing out the shortcomings of each when used in isolation. He argues that while a long-term strategy is necessary, it is not sufficient without the appropriate tactical execution.

[Translator's Note]

In a business context, this insight speaks to the need for a balanced approach between long-term strategic planning and day-to-day operational tactics. A business might have an ambitious vision (strategy) but needs well-planned operational plans (tactics) to realize it. Similarly, even the best day-to-day operations will fall short without a strategic vision guiding them.

«Appear weak when you are strong, and strong when you are weak.» - Sun Tzu

Sun Tzu highlights the importance of managing perceptions in warfare. It's a psychological strategy meant to deceive the enemy.

[Translator's Note]

In business, this principle could apply to competitive strategy and negotiations. Companies may choose to understate their strengths to avoid attracting competition or overstate them when they are vulnerable to deter threats. The careful management of external perceptions can be a powerful strategic tool in a competitive landscape.

The teachings of Sun Tzu continue to provide modern businesses with valuable insights into strategic and tactical planning, as well as the management of perceptions. Whether navigating the complexities of organizational operations or facing competitive pressures in the market, leaders can apply these ancient yet timeless principles to guide their decision-making processes.

«The supreme art of war is to subdue the enemy without fighting.» - Sun Tzu

Sun Tzu presents his ultimate strategy of war here: to achieve victory without engaging in actual combat. This principle emphasizes the power of diplomacy, negotiation, and psychological warfare.

[Translator's Note]

In business, this wisdom could be interpreted as achieving market leadership or outperforming competitors without resorting to direct confrontation or price wars. It underscores the power of innovative products, brand building, customer loyalty, and other strategies that can help a company surpass its competition without necessarily engaging in direct confrontations.

«Rouse him, and learn the principle of his activity or inactivity. Force him to reveal himself, so as to find out his vulnerable spots.» - Sun Tzu

Sun Tzu suggests that provoking an enemy can reveal their patterns and weaknesses, valuable information for strategic planning.

[Translator's Note]

In a business context, this could be seen as encouraging market competition to understand a competitor's strategy and weaknesses. It could also refer to market research techniques used to understand customer behavior. The information derived from these techniques helps businesses create effective strategies and products.

Sun Tzu's principles continue to offer valuable lessons for businesses today, from winning without fighting to understanding competitors' vulnerabilities. The application of these insights can lead to powerful strategies that provide a competitive edge, underlining the relevance of Sun Tzu's wisdom in today's business world.

«Opportunities multiply as they are seized.» - Sun Tzu

Sun Tzu asserts here that taking advantage of opportunities as they arise leads to the creation of even more opportunities. This principle suggests a domino effect in opportunities created by proactive actions.

[Translator's Note]

For businesses, this quote emphasizes the importance of capitalizing on opportunities as they come and the potential chain effect of doing so. For instance, a successful product launch can open up opportunities for extensions, partnerships, or entering new markets. This quote suggests a proactive, opportunistic business strategy.

«When strong, avoid them. If of high morale, depress them. Seem humble to fill them with conceit. If at ease, exhaust them. If united, separate them.» - Sun Tzu

This quote from Sun Tzu provides a list of strategies to gain an advantage over opponents based on their current condition.

[Translator's Note]

In business, these tactics could be applied in various ways. For example, if a competitor is strong in a certain area, it may be wise to avoid direct competition in that area and instead focus on their weaknesses. If a competitor is complacent, a company could introduce an innovative product to disrupt the market. If competitors are collaborating, measures could be taken to disrupt that alliance.

Sun Tzu's wisdom remains as applicable in today's business environment as it was in ancient warfare. The strategic seizing of opportunities and nuanced approach to dealing with competitors provide useful lessons for modern businesses seeking a competitive edge.

«In the midst of chaos, there is also opportunity.» - Sun Tzu

Sun Tzu asserts that even within a state of disarray or uncertainty, opportunities for success can be found. This perspective emphasizes adaptability and resilience in the face of adversity.

[Translator's Note]

From a business standpoint, this can be interpreted as the potential for growth and innovation in times of disruption or industry change. For example, many businesses have used economic downturns or technological disruptions as opportunities to pivot their business models, introduce innovative solutions, or tap into new markets.

«Let your plans be dark and impenetrable as night, and when you move, fall like a thunderbolt.» - Sun Tzu

Here, Sun Tzu advises keeping strategies and plans hidden from enemies until the moment of action, at which point the actions should be swift and powerful.

[Translator's Note]

In the corporate world, this wisdom can translate to businesses keeping their strategies and upcoming products or services confidential until the moment of launch. The surprise factor can create significant market buzz and potentially disrupt competitors, giving the business a competitive advantage.

These two aphorisms highlight Sun Tzu's understanding of opportunities that arise from chaos and the power of strategic secrecy in achieving victory. These principles continue to inform modern business strategies, emphasizing resilience in the face of disruption and the element of surprise in competitive markets.

«Pretend inferiority and encourage his arrogance.» - Sun Tzu

Sun Tzu recommends displaying a façade of weakness to encourage the enemy's overconfidence, which could lead to their downfall. This is a psychological strategy used to gain an advantage.

[Translator's Note]

In a business context, this principle could apply to competitive strategy. By downplaying strengths, a company may lead competitors to underestimate them. This could be a strategic move to deter competitors from replicating business strategies or to surprise the market with unexpected innovations or expansions.

«Even the finest sword plunged into salt water will eventually rust.» - Sun Tzu

Sun Tzu cautions against complacency, emphasizing that even the most formidable forces or strategies can deteriorate if not properly maintained or adapted to changing circumstances.

[Translator's Note]

For businesses, this wisdom serves as a reminder of the importance of continual improvement and adaptation. Regardless of current success, businesses must continue to innovate, adapt, and stay vigilant to maintain their edge and stay relevant in the marketplace.

These insights from Sun Tzu continue to resonate in today's business environment. The tactics of displaying modesty to outmaneuver competitors, and the warning against complacency, offer timeless wisdom for modern businesses navigating the complex dynamics of competitive markets.

«If your enemy is secure at all points, be prepared for him. If he is in superior strength, evade him.» - Sun Tzu

Sun Tzu advises on how to deal with a well-prepared or stronger enemy. He suggests preparing well for a secure enemy and avoiding direct confrontation with a stronger one.

[Translator's Note]

For businesses, this insight can translate into competitive strategies. If a competitor is well-established and has a strong market position, it may be more effective to find unique market niches or innovate rather than directly challenging them. This approach allows businesses to build their own strengths and customer base without engaging in direct competition.

«There is no instance of a nation benefitting from prolonged warfare.» - Sun Tzu

Sun Tzu warns against drawn-out conflicts, stating that they often lead to significant losses rather than benefits.

[Translator's Note]

In the business world, this can be seen as a caution against engaging in long-term, direct competition that drains resources. Instead, businesses may find more success in focusing on growth, development, and building a solid customer base. Collaborative strategies like partnerships and alliances can also be beneficial alternatives to ongoing rivalry.

These teachings from Sun Tzu provide valuable insights for modern businesses. They offer guidance on handling competition, highlighting the importance of unique market positioning and strategic growth over prolonged direct competition.

«He will win who, prepared himself, waits to take the enemy unprepared.» - Sun Tzu

Sun Tzu highlights the advantage of readiness and patience in strategy, emphasizing the benefit of striking when the enemy least expects it.

From a business standpoint, this stresses the importance of strategic planning and patience. Companies that take the time to carefully plan their strategies, while keeping an eye on the market and competitors, are often better equipped to seize opportunities when they arise.

[Translator's Note]

This again emphasizes the need for a full perspective in business. A company might see an opportunity to disrupt a market or launch a new product, but if it doesn't consider its own readiness—in terms of resources, personnel, infrastructure, or other necessary conditions—it could lead to failure. Thus, self-awareness and market awareness are both essential for strategic planning.

«Supreme excellence consists in breaking the enemy's resistance without fighting.» - Sun Tzu

Sun Tzu points out that the most excellent victory is one where you overcome your enemy without even needing to fight, suggesting the power of strategic and psychological warfare.

[Translator's Note]

In the realm of business, this could mean achieving market dominance or outperforming competitors through superior strategy, innovative products or services, or better understanding of customer needs, without engaging in destructive price wars or aggressive marketing campaigns.

Through these aphorisms, Sun Tzu provides valuable insights into the importance of strategic patience and the potential to achieve victory without direct confrontation. These lessons can serve modern businesses in navigating their competitive landscapes, highlighting the effectiveness of careful planning and the power of strategic innovation.

«In the midst of chaos, there is also opportunity.» - Sun Tzu

Sun Tzu asserts that even within a state of disarray or uncertainty, opportunities for success can be found. This perspective emphasizes adaptability and resilience in the face of adversity.

[Translator's Note]

From a business standpoint, this can be interpreted as the potential for growth and innovation in times of disruption or industry change. For example, many businesses have used economic downturns or technological disruptions as opportunities to pivot their business models, introduce innovative solutions, or tap into new markets.

«The supreme art of war is to subdue the enemy without fighting.» - Sun Tzu

Sun Tzu suggests that the greatest victory is achieving your objectives without needing to engage in actual combat, highlighting the importance of strategy and diplomacy.

[Translator's Note]

In business terms, this can mean winning market share, achieving growth, or surpassing competitors through strategic planning, negotiation, or by offering superior products and services, rather than through more confrontational means like price wars or aggressive marketing.

These quotes reflect Sun Tzu's understanding of how to turn chaos into opportunity and how to achieve victory through strategy and diplomacy. His insights can still offer valuable lessons for modern business strategists, emphasizing the need for resilience, strategic planning, and the ability to find opportunities in challenging situations.

«The opportunity to secure ourselves against defeat lies in our own hands, but the opportunity of defeating the enemy is provided by the enemy himself.» - Sun Tzu

Sun Tzu underscores the idea that control over our own defenses is essential, but the chances to overcome the enemy often come from the enemy's own mistakes or oversights.

[Translator's Note]

In a business context, this suggests that while companies can control their own strategies and defenses, opportunities to outdo competitors often arise from the competitors' missteps. For instance, a competitor may overlook a key market trend, allowing your business to step in and fill the gap.

«Victorious warriors win first and then go to war, while defeated warriors go to war first and then seek to win.» - Sun Tzu

Sun Tzu emphasizes the importance of preparation and strategy, stating that victory is achieved before the battle begins, through superior planning and foresight.

[Translator's Note]

This insight is particularly relevant in business strategy, where successful companies often win by thoroughly researching the market, understanding customer needs, and developing an effective business strategy before launching a product or entering a new market.

These aphorisms underline the importance of strategic preparation and the ability to seize opportunities from competitors' errors. Sun Tzu's wisdom continues to be applicable in the business world, reminding us of the value of forethought, strategy, and vigilance.

«The general who wins the battle makes many calculations in his temple before the battle is fought. The general who loses makes but few calculations beforehand.» - Sun Tzu

Sun Tzu emphasizes that careful planning and anticipation of various outcomes are key to victory, while hasty, unplanned actions often lead to defeat.

[Translator's Note]

In business terms, this principle underscores the value of thorough market research, strategic planning, and risk management before making major decisions. Whether launching a new product, entering a new market, or investing in a new technology, comprehensive preparation is crucial for success.

«Speed is the essence of war. Take advantage of the enemy's unpreparedness; travel by unexpected routes and strike him where he has taken no precautions.» - Sun Tzu

Sun Tzu emphasizes the element of surprise and quick action in strategy, recommending capitalizing on the enemy's unpreparedness.

[Translator's Note]

For businesses, speed and agility can be competitive advantages, allowing them to adapt quickly to market changes, seize new opportunities, or respond to competitors' actions. However, speed must be coupled with strategic insight to ensure that quick actions lead to desired outcomes.

Sun Tzu's principles of careful calculation and speed in strategy offer valuable insights for business strategies. They highlight the importance of meticulous planning and the ability to quickly seize opportunities, providing timeless guidance for navigating competitive markets.

«If you know the enemy and know yourself, you need not fear the result of a hundred battles.» - Sun Tzu

Sun Tzu underscores the importance of thorough understanding of both oneself and the enemy. With such knowledge, fear of loss diminishes, as you can anticipate and effectively counter the enemy's tactics.

[Translator's Note]

In business terms, this reflects the necessity of deep market research and self-awareness. Companies need to understand their own strengths and weaknesses, as well as those of their competitors, to strategically position themselves in the market and anticipate potential threats and opportunities.

.

«Even the finest sword plunged into salt water will eventually rust.» - Sun Tzu

Sun Tzu draws attention to the fact that even the best tools or strategies will degrade if left in unsuitable conditions for too long.

[Translator's Note]

In the business world, this aphorism might suggest that even the best products, services, or business models need to be regularly updated and adapted to the changing market environment to remain effective. Stagnation or neglect can lead to deterioration and loss of competitive edge.

These quotes from Sun Tzu serve as reminders of the importance of self-knowledge and adaptability in strategic planning. They illustrate the value of understanding oneself and one's competitors and the need for constant evolution to maintain a competitive edge in the ever-changing business landscape.

«In the practical art of war, the best thing of all is to take the enemy's country whole and intact; to shatter and destroy it is not so good.» - Sun Tzu

Sun Tzu asserts the value of preserving the integrity of conquered territory rather than ravaging it. A destroyed territory is of no use; a preserved one can yield many benefits.

[Translator's Note]

In business, this can be seen in practices like mergers and acquisitions. The goal is often to retain the useful elements of the acquired company (like technology, talent, customer base, or brand reputation) rather than to dismantle it entirely. In essence, it's about building upon and benefiting from what is already there, rather than destroying and starting afresh.

«Appear weak when you are strong, and strong when you are weak.» - Sun Tzu

Sun Tzu advocates for deceptive strategy, suggesting that seeming vulnerable when you're capable can lead enemies into a trap, and appearing robust when you're weak can deter potential threats.

[Translator's Note]

In a business context, this could be interpreted as strategic positioning or even bluffing. Companies might downplay their strengths to keep competitors off guard or exaggerate their capabilities to discourage competitive threats. However, such strategies should be used judiciously and ethically.

These teachings from Sun Tzu touch on the principles of preservation and deception in strategy, revealing further layers of strategic depth that can be applied in modern business scenarios. These insights encourage thoughtful consideration of all the available resources and careful manipulation of perception to gain a competitive edge.

«The supreme art of war is to subdue the enemy without fighting.» - Sun Tzu

Sun Tzu believes that the highest form of warfare is to conquer the enemy without even needing to fight. This can be achieved through superior strategy, diplomacy, or psychological tactics.

[Translator's Note]

In business, this could be analogous to winning market share or outperforming competitors not just through head-to-head competition, but through superior innovation, brand positioning, customer service, or other non-confrontational strategies. The goal is to make your business such an attractive option that customers choose you over your competitors, effectively 'defeating' them without a 'battle'.

«He who is prudent and lies in wait for an enemy who is not, will be victorious.» - Sun Tzu

Sun Tzu emphasizes the importance of patience, caution, and timing in achieving victory. Waiting for the right opportunity can often yield better results than rushing into action.

[Translator's Note]

In the business context, this might suggest the importance of strategic patience. Companies should not rush into markets or launch products until they have thoroughly prepared and the timing is right. This could mean waiting for technological advancements, market readiness, or a lull in competitive activity.

Sun Tzu's teachings on avoiding unnecessary conflict and the value of strategic patience offer critical lessons for business strategies. They stress the importance of non-aggressive methods of outperforming competitors and the need for careful timing in business decisions.

«In the midst of chaos, there is also opportunity.» - Sun Tzu

Sun Tzu recognizes that amidst disorder and uncertainty, there also lies a chance for advantage. Chaos can disrupt the status quo, providing openings for those ready to seize them.

[Translator's Note]

In a business context, periods of market disruption or industry turmoil can indeed create new opportunities. Companies that are agile and innovative can exploit these circumstances to introduce new products, capture new customer segments, or otherwise gain a competitive edge.

«Treat your men as you would your own beloved sons. And they will follow you into the deepest valley.» - Sun Tzu

Sun Tzu highlights the importance of good leadership and the value of treating those under one's command with care and respect.

[Translator's Note]

In modern business, this principle resonates with the importance of good management and employee relations. Employees who feel valued and respected are more likely to be motivated, productive, and loyal to the company. This, in turn, contributes to a more harmonious and effective work environment.

These quotes from Sun Tzu emphasize the potential benefits of chaos and the significance of treating your team well. Both of these insights can be applied to contemporary business strategy, underscoring the need to see opportunity in disruption and the importance of maintaining positive employee relations.

«Victorious warriors win first and then go to war, while defeated warriors go to war first and then seek to win.» - Sun Tzu

Sun Tzu underscores the importance of preparation and planning. Victory is secured before the battle begins, through careful strategy, not during the heat of the conflict.

[Translator's Note]

In a business context, this emphasizes the importance of strategic planning. Successful companies do not dive headfirst into markets or initiatives without thorough research, planning, and preparation. A well-developed strategy acts as a roadmap to victory.

«He will win who, prepared himself, waits to take the enemy unprepared.» - Sun Tzu

Again, Sun Tzu emphasizes the importance of being prepared and the advantage it gives over unprepared adversaries. Readiness coupled with patience often leads to victory.

[Translator's Note]

For businesses, this could be interpreted as the importance of continuously improving processes, products, and services while also staying aware of the competitive landscape. This allows a company to seize opportunities when competitors are unprepared, thereby gaining a significant advantage..

Sun Tzu's wisdom reinforces the value of preparation and patience in strategy, whether it's in warfare or business. By investing time in planning and waiting for the opportune moment, one can secure an edge over less prepared competitors. This remains true even in the fast-paced world of modern business.

«All warfare is based on deception. Hence, when able to attack, we must seem unable; when using our forces, we must seem inactive; when we are near, we must make the enemy believe we are far away; when far away, we must make him believe we are near.» - Sun Tzu

Sun Tzu advocates the extensive use of misdirection and illusion in warfare. By making the enemy misjudge your abilities, intentions, and positions, you can gain a significant advantage.

[Translator's Note]

In business, while ethical considerations must always come first, there's still room for strategy and discretion. Companies often need to be discreet about new product developments, strategic initiatives, or business moves to avoid tipping off competitors. Misdirection can be used in competitive strategy, such as by publicly emphasizing one aspect of the business while privately investing in another.

«The general who wins a battle makes many calculations in his temple before the battle is fought. The general who loses a battle makes but few calculations beforehand.» - Sun Tzu

Sun Tzu highlights the critical role of planning and foresight in winning battles. Those who adequately prepare and plan are more likely to achieve victory.

[Translator's Note]

This principle translates directly into business strategy. Success often hinges on meticulous planning, including market research, financial analysis, risk assessment, and contingency planning. Companies that neglect this planning are more likely to fail or underperform.

These teachings from Sun Tzu touch on the principles of deception and detailed planning in strategy, providing additional depth for strategic considerations in modern business environments. They underscore the importance of planning and the judicious use of information in gaining a competitive advantage.

«Know thy self, know thy enemy. A thousand battles, a thousand victories.» - Sun Tzu

Sun Tzu states that self-knowledge and knowledge of the enemy lead to victory. Understanding your own strengths and weaknesses, as well as those of your adversary, is key to winning battles.

[Translator's Note]

In a business context, this quote emphasizes the importance of a company understanding its own capabilities, resources, and weaknesses, as well as those of its competitors. This kind of strategic analysis (often encapsulated in a SWOT analysis—Strengths, Weaknesses, Opportunities, Threats) is crucial to success in business.

«If you know the enemy and know yourself, you need not fear the result of a hundred battles.» - Sun Tzu

Again, Sun Tzu emphasizes the value of knowing oneself and the enemy. With this knowledge, one can face any challenge without fear.

[Translator's Note]

For businesses, this underscores the importance of market research and competitor analysis. By having a deep understanding of the market and your competitors, a company can better position its products or services, differentiate itself, and anticipate potential challenges or threats.

Sun Tzu's wisdom on the value of knowledge—both self-knowledge and knowledge of the adversary—is directly applicable to the business world. Comprehensive understanding of a company's own capabilities and those of its competitors is a key factor in shaping effective strategies and making sound business decisions.

«Strategy without tactics is the slowest route to victory. Tactics without strategy is the noise before defeat.» - Sun Tzu

Sun Tzu underlines the need for both strategy (the overall plan) and tactics (the specific actions taken to fulfill the plan). A balance between the two is vital for achieving victory swiftly and effectively.

[Translator's Note]

In business, strategy refers to the long-term plan or vision of where a company wants to go, while tactics are the day-to-day actions it takes to get there. Both are necessary for success. A brilliant vision with no implementation plan is unlikely to be realized, while a flurry of activity with no guiding strategy often leads to wasted resources and potential failure.

«In the practical art of war, the best thing of all is to take the enemy's country whole and intact; to shatter and destroy it is not so good.» - Sun Tzu

Sun Tzu suggests that the optimal victory is one that leaves the enemy's resources intact for your own use, rather than destroying them in the process of conquest.

[Translator's Note]

In modern business, this could be seen in the way companies approach mergers and acquisitions. The aim is often to acquire companies that complement or enhance the acquiring company's capabilities, rather than dismantling them. The value of a company often lies not just in its tangible assets, but in its personnel, brand, technology, or customer base.

Sun Tzu's words on the balance between strategy and tactics and the importance of preserving value in conquest provide valuable insights for business strategy. A blend of long-term vision and day-to-day execution, along with a focus on value preservation in acquisitions, are key considerations for modern businesses.

«He will win who knows when to fight and when not to fight.»
- Sun Tzu

Sun Tzu advises that choosing the right moment to engage in battle is just as important as the battle tactics themselves. Knowing when to back off or avoid confrontation can be as vital to success as knowing when to push forward.

[Translator's Note]

In a business context, this suggests the importance of timing in strategic decisions. Knowing when to launch a product, when to enter or exit a market, or when to compete or collaborate can be crucial for success. Choosing the wrong time for these actions can lead to missed opportunities or unnecessary risk.

«The supreme art of war is to subdue the enemy without fighting.» - Sun Tzu

Sun Tzu proposes that the highest form of warfare is not to engage in physical battle at all but rather to win through strategy alone.

[Translator's Note]

In business, this is akin to winning market share not through aggressive tactics like price wars, but through superior strategy - for instance, better product design, superior customer service, or innovative business models. It highlights the power of non-confrontational strategies in achieving business objectives.

Sun Tzu's wisdom on knowing when to engage and the supremacy of non-confrontational victory provides valuable lessons for business strategy. The art of timing and the power of strategic, rather than aggressive, methods can be game-changers in the competitive landscape of business.

«He who knows the aspects of the battlefield will always be victorious.» - Sun Tzu

Sun Tzu underlines the importance of understanding one's environment and circumstances before engaging in a battle.

[Translator's Note]

This correlates to market research in a business context. Understanding the competitive landscape, customer needs, and economic trends are vital for business success.

«The general who does not advance to seek glory, or does not withdraw to avoid punishment, but cares for only the people's security and promotes the people's interests, is the nation's treasure.» - Sun Tzu

Sun Tzu suggests that a true leader prioritizes the welfare of the people above personal gain.

[Translator's Note]

In business, leaders who prioritize the well-being of their employees and stakeholders often foster loyalty and drive long-term success. This also underscores the value of ethical leadership.

This concludes Chapter 10, «The Terrain» or «Situational Positioning,» where Sun Tzu emphasizes understanding the 'terrain' and selfless, ethical leadership. Both concepts find resonance in today's business world.

CHAPTER 11: The Nine Situations

Sun Tzu's discussion of the nine situations of warfare provides crucial insight into the art of strategic planning. Let's translate these battle scenarios into a modern business context:

1. Dispersive Ground: When we're comfortable and secure in our own territory, the risk of complacency arises. In business, this could mean losing touch with our competitive edge if we rely too much on our existing market dominance. Our strategy must evolve with market dynamics to maintain our leadership position.

2. Facile Ground: A bit of progress into enemy territory presents us with a new market segment or a new product development. However, the journey is just beginning. Retreat is not an option, but reckless advance may expose us to greater risks. We must cautiously but steadily push forward.

3. Contentious Ground: Possessing value or resources that rivals covet. In business, this may be a proprietary technology, a key talent, or a valuable partnership. Protect these resources and leverage them to your advantage.

4. Open Ground: An open market, ripe for the taking, but with no clear winner. Innovation and a strong understanding of customer needs can provide a competitive edge.

5. Ground of Intersecting Highways: These are sectors of strategic importance, where competition is intense. It's a game of alliances here, partnerships can tip the scales of success.

6. Serious Ground: Ventures where a high level of commitment is required. Once a company has invested significant resources, it must ensure maximum returns. This could involve anything from a merger and acquisition to an ambitious product launch.

7. Difficult Ground: Market situations or projects fraught with challenges and risks. In such scenarios, persistence, agility, and careful risk management are key.

8. Hemmed-in Ground: Situations where a company is caught in a tricky situation, possibly a harsh regulatory environment or a competitive bind. Creativity and innovation are the way out.

9. Desperate Ground: Do-or-die scenarios where the stakes are highest. The company's survival may be at stake. In such situations, courage, resourcefulness, and resilience are key. Strategy should be about endurance and transformation.

Each 'ground' or situation, as Sun Tzu presented, is a reflection of different business scenarios. As business leaders, recognizing the ground we're on and adapting our strategies accordingly can be the difference between success and failure.

CHAPTER 12: The Attack by Fire

Fire, in Sun Tzu's time, was a formidable tool in warfare. The essence of its use was rooted in its ability to cause damage, chaos, and destruction in enemy camps, weakening them significantly. In today's business world, we can extrapolate this as being a disruptive strategy that radically transforms the competitive landscape.

1. The Five Ways of Attacking with Fire: In business, 'fire' can represent different strategies aimed at disrupting the competition or gaining a distinct advantage. Sun Tzu described five ways of attacking with fire, each with its contemporary equivalent:

a. Burning Personnel: Sun Tzu was referring to affecting the enemy's manpower. In business, this could translate to strategies aimed at winning over the competitor's key employees or affecting their morale.

b. Burning Supplies: In the context of modern business, this could refer to strategies aimed at disrupting the competitor's supply chain or source of resources.

c. Burning Equipment: In Sun Tzu's time, this was about destroying the enemy's weapons. Today, it could symbolize strategies aimed at making the competitor's technology or tools obsolete.

d. Burning Stores: This entailed setting the enemy's stockpiles on fire. In the business world, it could be about outdoing the competitor's product line or services.

e. Using Incendiary Weapons: In business terms, this can be equated with strategies that cause market-wide disruptions, forcing competitors to change their approach.

The essence of 'Attack by Fire' is not about literal destruction but about disrupting the status quo in a way that provides a competitive advantage. As businesses adapt to the fast-paced world, they must learn to 'light fires' that can illuminate their path to success.

2. Appropriate Timing and Calculation: Just as how in ancient warfare, the success of an attack by fire depended on weather conditions and timing, so too does the success of disruptive strategies in business. Understanding the market, its trends, and the competitor's position is crucial to determining the right time to introduce a disruption.

a. Understanding the Market: Sun Tzu stressed understanding the terrain and weather. Similarly, businesses need to grasp the complexities of their market. This includes staying updated with industry trends, understanding customer behavior and preferences, and being aware of regulatory changes.

b. Calculating Risks: A fire can turn into a friend or foe, depending on the wind direction. Likewise, disruptive strategies come with inherent risks. Companies need to conduct a thorough risk assessment before proceeding. This can include financial risk, reputational risk, operational risk, and more.

3. Adaptive Strategies: Sun Tzu believed in adapting strategies based on situations. In today's dynamic business world, sticking to rigid plans can be detrimental. Organizations need to be flexible in their approach, adapting to the changing circumstances.

4. Ethical Considerations: While Sun Tzu advocated the use of fire, he also warned against unnecessary cruelty. In business, while competitiveness is necessary, ethics should not be compromised. Fair play, corporate social responsibility, and ethical considerations should be central to a company's strategies.

As we navigate through the ever-changing business landscape, Sun Tzu's strategies on 'Attack by Fire' remind us of the importance of being disruptive, calculative, adaptive, and ethical in our approach. Each 'fire' we light should aim to illuminate our path, not burn the bridge for others. Remember, in the long run, businesses that play fair and contribute positively to their environment are the ones that succeed and are respected.

CHAPTER 13: The Use of Spies

Espionage, or the use of spies, was an important aspect of Sun Tzu's strategic thought. It helped obtain information about the enemy, which in turn informed the planning and execution of war strategies. In the business world, this translates to gathering competitive intelligence, a practice that is both legal and ethical when done correctly.

1. The Importance of Competitive Intelligence: In a hyper-competitive business landscape, information is power. Knowing what your competitors are up to - their strategies, strengths, weaknesses, and plans - can provide a significant competitive edge. This doesn't mean crossing ethical boundaries but rather engaging in diligent market research, customer feedback, and observation.

2. Types of Spies: Sun Tzu identified five types of spies. In a modern business context, these could be interpreted as follows:

a. Local spies: These are akin to your customers, suppliers, or other entities who interact with your competitors as well. They provide valuable feedback and insights.

b. Inward spies: These could be employees of your competitors who may unknowingly reveal useful information about their employers.

c. Converted spies: These are competitors' employees who intentionally provide you with information. It's crucial to note that inducing someone to betray their employer is both unethical and illegal.

d. Doomed spies: In the business context, these are disinformation agents, who may spread false information about your company to mislead competitors.

e. Surviving spies: These could be your employees who interact with the competition in industry events, trade fairs, etc., and come back with useful information.

3. Ethical Considerations: While gathering competitive intelligence is critical, it's equally important to ensure that the methods used are legal and ethical. Breaching privacy, inducing someone to break confidentiality agreements, or spreading false information are unacceptable practices.

4. Utilizing Intelligence: The purpose of gathering intelligence is to inform your strategic decisions. This information should be carefully analyzed and used to predict competitors' moves, identify opportunities, and avoid potential threats.

In conclusion, Sun Tzu's Art of War offers timeless wisdom that can be applied to various spheres of life, including business. The lessons derived from the strategies of ancient warfare can be adapted to the modern business landscape, offering invaluable insights for success and sustainability. Whether it is about being agile, employing disruptive tactics, or gathering competitive intelligence, the teachings from this ancient text continue to remain relevant and instructive.

CHAPTER 14: The Art of Adaptation

In war and in business, as in life, change is the only constant. Sun Tzu emphasized the importance of adapting strategies to meet evolving circumstances. This ability to adapt and evolve is the very essence of survival, and it is a principle that businesses must understand and implement.

1. Understanding Change: Sun Tzu believed that the art of war was of vital importance to the state, a matter of life and death. In the business context, this can be translated as the understanding that change - whether in the form of evolving market trends, consumer behaviors, technologies, or regulations - is an essential aspect of the business landscape that can dramatically affect a company's survival and prosperity.

2. Anticipating Change: Just as a successful general anticipates the movements of his enemy, a successful business needs to foresee changes in the business landscape. This involves not only staying updated with industry trends and news, but also predicting future shifts through market research and analysis.

3. Embracing Change: Resistance to change can lead to stagnation and decline. Businesses must be willing to embrace change, however uncomfortable it may be. This can involve adopting new technologies, entering new markets, adjusting business models, and even redefining company mission and values when necessary.

4. Driving Change: Sun Tzu said, «In the midst of chaos, there is also opportunity». Businesses that take proactive steps to drive change, rather than just react to it, can gain a competitive advantage. This involves innovation, disruption, and leadership.ability to find opportunities in challenging situations.

5. Building a Culture of Adaptation: Adapting to change isn't just a strategic consideration; it also involves fostering a culture that values flexibility, resilience, learning, and innovation. This can include developing adaptive leadership, investing in continuous learning and development, encouraging innovative thinking, and cultivating resilience in the face of setbacks and failures.

Adaptation is a journey, not a destination. As we continue to navigate the complex and ever-evolving business landscape, the principles of the Art of War can provide guidance and insights to help us embrace, anticipate, and even drive change, while maintaining our focus on the ultimate goal: achieving sustainable success.

CHAPTER 15: The Use of Spies

Spies, or the gathering of intelligence, played an integral role in Sun Tzu's approach to warfare. Applied to the business world, this translates to the necessity of comprehensive market research, competitive analysis, and a deep understanding of the industry landscape.

1. The Importance of Information: Knowledge is power in warfare, as well as in business. Making informed decisions is crucial to maintain a competitive edge. This information can range from understanding the competition's strategies and weaknesses, knowing consumer behavior and preferences, or being aware of upcoming regulatory changes.

2. Methods of Gathering Intelligence: In today's digital age, businesses have a plethora of tools at their disposal for gathering market intelligence. These can include traditional methods like surveys and focus groups, as well as advanced techniques like social listening, web analytics, and AI-powered data mining.

3. Analyzing Information: Collecting information is only half the battle. The real value lies in analyzing this information to generate actionable insights. Businesses should invest in data analysis skills and tools to make sense of the vast amount of data that they collect.

4. Protecting Your Information: Just as important as gathering information about others, is protecting your own business intelligence from prying eyes. This involves robust cybersecurity measures, strong internal policies about information sharing, and maintaining the confidentiality of strategic plans.

5. Ethical Considerations: While gathering information about competitors is essential, it's equally important to do so ethically and legally. Spying in the traditional sense has no place in a respectful business environment. Competitive intelligence should be gathered through publicly available sources, industry analysis, and ethical practices.

In the Art of War, Sun Tzu teaches us that winning a battle is not just about physical strength, but also about outsmarting the enemy. This lesson continues to be applicable in today's business world, where companies that can gather, analyze, and apply information effectively will have a strategic advantage. In the next chapter, we will explore more on applying these strategies to specific business functions.

CHAPTER 16: The Strategy in Action Marketing and Sales

Taking the lessons from the Art of War, we apply the strategies of Sun Tzu to two of the key functions of any business - Marketing and Sales.

1. Knowing the Market (Terrain): Just like how a commander should know the battleground, a business must know its market. This includes understanding customer demographics, preferences, buying habits, and key market trends.

2. Competitive Positioning (Formations): Understanding where your business stands relative to its competitors is essential. Are you a market leader, a challenger, a niche player, or a new entrant? Your marketing and sales strategies should reflect your market position.

3. Unique Value Proposition (Fire Attack): Your business should have a unique value proposition that sets it apart from its competitors. This is your 'fire attack' - the aspect of your product or service that can deliver a critical blow to your competitors.

4. Customer Engagement (The Empty Castle): Just like the 'empty castle' strategy where an enemy is lured into an empty fortress, businesses need to engage customers and keep them interested. This can be through exceptional customer service, engaging marketing campaigns, or loyalty programs.

5. Persuasion and Influence (Chain Reactions): The 'chain reaction' strategy involves creating a momentum that the enemy cannot resist. In marketing and sales, this can be likened to creating a 'buzz' or hype around your product or service that makes customers want to buy.

6. Adjusting to Market Changes (Adaptive Strategy): Just like a battlefield, the market is not static. It changes constantly. Businesses must be ready to adapt their marketing and sales strategies based on these changes.

By applying the strategies of Sun Tzu in marketing and sales, a business can gain a competitive edge, win over customers, and achieve market success. In the next chapter, we explore how these strategies apply to Human Resources and Leadership.

CHAPTER 17: Human Resources
and Leadership

In this chapter, we apply Sun Tzu's wisdom to the critical business areas of Human Resources and Leadership.

1. Talent Management (Terrain): A battlefield's terrain shapes a military campaign, just as a company's talent shapes its strategic success. Understanding your personnel's strengths and weaknesses is key to allocating roles and responsibilities effectively.

2. Leadership Styles (Formations): Different situations call for different leadership styles. An effective leader, like an effective commander, adjusts their approach based on the context, be it directive, supportive, participatory, or achievement-oriented.

3. Building a Strong Culture (Fire Attack): A cohesive, positive company culture is akin to the 'fire attack,' fostering a sense of purpose, unity, and motivation that can drive significant business success.

4. Employee Engagement (The Empty Castle): Engagement is crucial for retaining talent. By keeping employees engaged through clear communication, recognition, and opportunities for growth, companies can minimize the risk of talent attrition.

5. Leadership Influence (Chain Reactions): Leaders set the tone and direction for the organization. Their decisions and behaviors can trigger 'chain reactions' that profoundly impact team morale and productivity.

6. Adaptive Leadership (Adaptive Strategy): The business environment is ever-changing. Leaders must adapt their strategies based on shifting market dynamics, technological innovations, and workforce changes.

In the next chapter, we will explore the application of Sun Tzu's strategies to Finance and Operations.

CHAPTER 18: Finance and Operations

Turning our attention to Finance and Operations, Sun Tzu's wisdom still holds relevance in these fundamental aspects of business.

1. Resource Management (The Army on the March): Proper resource allocation, be it financial, human, or physical, is akin to marching an army. Missteps can lead to exhaustion of resources and eventual failure.

2. Financial Planning (Estimating the Enemy): A company must plan and forecast its finances like a general gauging the enemy's strength. Not only will this help avoid financial pitfalls, but it will also provide a strategic edge in a competitive market.

3. Operational Efficiency (Formations): Operations, like military formations, must be flexible yet structured, ensuring efficiency and adaptability in varying business situations.

4. Risk Management (Terrain): Just as the general considers the risks of the battlefield terrain, so too must a business assess financial and operational risks and develop appropriate mitigation strategies.

5. Value Chain Optimization (Fire Attack): Optimizing the value chain is akin to a well-executed fire attack. By improving the interconnected activities that create product value, companies can enhance profitability and customer satisfaction.

6. Cost Control (Supply Lines): Keeping costs under control is akin to managing supply lines in warfare. Excessive costs can 'starve' a company of its profits, similar to an army cut off from its provisions.

In the next chapter, we will dive into the application of Sun Tzu's wisdom in Innovation and Change Management.

CHAPTER 19: Innovation and Change Managemen

Sun Tzu's ancient wisdom also finds its place in the contemporary areas of Innovation and Change Management.

1. Fostering Innovation (Strategic Depth): Just as a general may need to adapt and change tactics during a campaign, businesses must continually innovate to stay competitive. It's about diving deeper into the market, understanding the undercurrents, and coming up with groundbreaking solutions.

2. Managing Change (The Army on the March): Like an army on the move, businesses undergoing change must maintain order and morale. Transparent communication, addressing concerns, and managing the pace of change are essential elements in this process.

3. Encouraging Creativity (Terrain): Creativity, like the terrain in warfare, can be the game-changer in business. Creating an environment that encourages creative thinking can lead to breakthrough ideas and solutions.

4. Navigating Market Changes (Estimating the Enemy): The market, like an adversary, can be unpredictable. Businesses need to stay agile, ready to adapt their strategies in response to shifts in consumer behavior, technological advancements, or competitive dynamics.

5. Change Resistance (The Empty Castle): Resistance to change is a common challenge in businesses. Leaders must anticipate this resistance and employ strategies to ease the transition, akin to the «empty castle» tactic.

6. Innovation Strategy (Chain Reactions): Innovation should be strategic, aligning with broader business objectives and triggering a positive chain reaction throughout the company, enhancing overall value proposition.

The final chapter will provide a summative discussion on the enduring relevance of Sun Tzu's principles in modern business.

CHAPTER 20: The Enduring Relevance of Sun Tzu's Art of War in Business

As we reach the end of our exploration, we reaffirm the timeless wisdom of Sun Tzu's Art of War and its applicability to the business world.

1. Timeless Wisdom (The Eternal Battlefield): Sun Tzu's strategies, formed thousands of years ago on the battlefields of ancient China, still hold relevance. They have transcended time and context, offering valuable insights to leaders in the 21st-century business landscape.

2. Broad Application (Terrain): The diversity of topics covered - from strategy and leadership to finance and innovation - demonstrates the broad applicability of Sun Tzu's teachings in various business domains.

3. Foresight (The Army on the March): Sun Tzu emphasized the importance of foresight in warfare. This principle is no less critical in business. Anticipating market changes, competitor moves, and technological advancements allows businesses to prepare and respond effectively.

4. Adaptability (Estimating the Enemy): Just as a general must adapt his strategies to the enemy's strength and position, so too must businesses adjust their strategies in the face of market dynamics and competitive pressures.

5. Holistic Approach (The Whole Army): Sun Tzu's Art of War encourages a holistic view, considering all aspects of the situation before making a move. In business, this translates into a comprehensive approach, considering all factors - internal and external - before making strategic decisions.

5. Holistic Approach (The Whole Army): Sun Tzu's Art of War encourages a holistic view, considering all aspects of the situation before making a move. In business, this translates into a comprehensive approach, considering all factors - internal and external - before making strategic decisions.

6. Enduring Principles (The Endless War): Lastly, the enduring nature of Sun Tzu's principles reminds us that, while tactics may change with time and technology, the underlying strategies of success remain constant.

In the end, Sun Tzu's Art of War is not just about war. It's about understanding the dynamics of competition, the importance of strategic planning, and the value of strong leadership. Its teachings are as relevant to the boardroom as they were to the ancient battlefields.

EPILOGUE: The Future of War and Business

Just as we have seen the wisdom of Sun Tzu find relevance in our modern era, so too can we expect it to continue providing valuable insights in the future.

1. Embracing Artificial Intelligence (The Master Strategist): As artificial intelligence and automation become increasingly prominent in business, Sun Tzu's teachings on strategy and foresight will guide leaders in leveraging these tools effectively and ethically.

2. Navigating Digital Warfare (The Battlefield Transformed): Cybersecurity, a modern equivalent to ancient warfare, also finds guidance in Sun Tzu's Art of War. Protecting sensitive information and maintaining digital integrity will be crucial.

3. Sustainability as a Strategy (The Earth Element): Sun Tzu's emphasis on the 'Earth' as a strategic element resonates with today's business focus on sustainability. Achieving harmony with the environment is now a strategic necessity and not just a competitive advantage.

4. Globalization (The All-Under-Heaven Perspective): As businesses operate in an increasingly interconnected world, the teachings of Sun Tzu can guide leaders in understanding the global landscape and crafting effective international strategies.

5. Future Leadership (The General's Evolution): The changing nature of work and society will demand different leadership skills. Still, Sun Tzu's leadership wisdom, emphasizing understanding, adaptability, and strategy, will continue to be pertinent.

As we step into an uncertain future, let us take with us the wisdom of the past. Sun Tzu's Art of War, once a guide for generals on the battlefield, now serves as a compass for leaders navigating the complex world of modern business. Its teachings, timeless and adaptable, will continue to enlighten and guide us, no matter what the future holds.

In every business, the victorious strategist only seeks battle after the victory has been won, whereas he who is destined to defeat first fights and afterwards looks for victory.

~Sun Tzu, The Art of War

AFTERWORD

It has been an enlightening journey to delve into the timeless wisdom of Sun Tzu's Art of War and explore its relevance in today's business world. Though the landscape of warfare and business has vastly transformed since Sun Tzu's time, the principles he laid down remain remarkably applicable.

In this era of rapid technological advancement, volatile markets, and ever-changing consumer behavior, the need for strategic thinking has never been more critical. As we have discovered through the course of this book, the teachings of Sun Tzu provide a profound guide for navigating these complex terrains.

It is our hope that this work provides a valuable resource for those seeking to understand and apply the principles of Sun Tzu in a contemporary context. May it serve as a compass in your strategic endeavors, shedding light on the path to victory in the face of uncertainty.

TABLE OF CONTENTS